ONLEY'S ARCTIC

DOUGLAS & McINTYRE
VANCOUVER / TORONTO

ONLEY'S ARCTIC

Diaries and Paintings of the High Arctic
TONI ONLEY

onley

CANADIAN CATALOGUING IN PUBLICATION DATA

Onley, Toni, 1928 –

Onley's Arctic

ISBN 0-88894-666-X

1. Onley, Toni, 1928 – Diaries. 2. Painters – British
Columbia – Diaries. 3. Onley, Toni, 1928 –
4. Arctic regions in art. I. Title.
ND249.055A2 1989 759.11 C89-091273-4

Douglas & McIntyre Ltd.
1615 Venables Street, Vancouver,
British Columbia, Canada V5L 2H1

Excerpt from *On Modern Art* by Paul Klee, translated by Paul
Findley (Faber & Faber Ltd., Publishers, 1984), © 1989, copyright
by COSMOPRESS, Geneva.

Excerpts from *A Painter's Country* by A. Y. Jackson (Clark, Irwin
& Co., 1967), are reprinted by permission of Stoddart Publishing.

Excerpt from *Concerning the Spiritual in Art* by Wassily
Kandinsky, 1977, reprinted by permission of the publisher, Dover
Publications, Inc.

Design and Typography: Reinhard Derreth Graphics Ltd.
Printing and Binding: C.S. Graphics Pte Ltd.
Printed and bound in Singapore

CONTENTS

In memory of
Maurice Haycock

Chosen are those artists who penetrate to the region of that secret place where primeval power nurtures all evolution.... Who is the artist that would not dwell there? In the womb of nature at the source of creation, where the secret key to all lies guarded.   Paul Klee, from *On Modern Art*

Cape Herschel
OIL, 1975

I am especially pleased to be introducing Toni Onley's diaries of his Arctic journeys because we have not only travelled together in the past but have also lived out important phases of our lives in the same distant places at different times. We were both in San Miguel de Allende in Mexico in the 1950s, though we did not encounter each other then. I was in the Arctic, in Keewatin, in 1968, six years before the first voyage recorded here; however, unlike Toni, I kept to the land and spent my time on the Barren Ground. The journeys that Toni and I made together took us to India and Europe, regions very different from the Arctic (though there must be something notably in common between painting Everest on a bitterly cold morning from a perch on Tiger Hill outside Darjeeling and painting an Arctic icescape from the crow's nest of an icebreaker).

There has, of course, been a transition in explorers' attitudes towards the Arctic since the Elizabethan and Jacobean voyagers went there during the first stage of the search for the Northwest Passage. The public attitude then was based on trade and politics, on the idea of opening a route to China that would be safe from the Spaniards, with the extra hope of finding gold on the way. These mariners were the first Europeans since the Icelanders to experience the perils of the northern seas, and the terrors of being trapped in the ice in little wooden ships of fifty and thirty-five tons, like those which John Davis sailed in 1595. Small wonder that, in an age with little sense of the sublime when men liked neat parks and loathed mountains, Davis's attitude should have been one of appalled negation.

> The lothsome view of the shore, and irksome noyze of the yce was such, as that it bred strange conceits among us, so that we supposed the place to be wast and voyd of any sensible or veritible creatures, whereupon I called the same Desolation.

The great wave of Arctic exploration came in the early nineteenth century. It too had its public aspects. The Napoleonic wars had ended; there were idle ships and officers in plenty, and exploration had acquired a prestige it retained through the nineteenth century until the last corners of the map were filled in. To brave the Arctic was a way of proving one's courage during the long century (devoid of major wars) between 1815 and 1914 when Britannia still more or less ruled the waves.

But there was also a different private sensibility at work compared with that of the Elizabethans, a sensibility tempered by Romanticism and by the cult of the sublime that by the end of the eighteenth century was transforming mountains and forests from horrid wastes into unspoilt Edens, and which inevitably had its effect on the ways in which men looked at the Arctic. One can see it in the difference in tone between the early seventeenth-century text of *The Strange and Dangerous Voyage of Captain Thomas James*, published in 1631, and the *Rime of the Ancient Mariner*, in which Coleridge paraphrased part of it almost two centuries later in 1798.

Coburg Island, Baffin Bay. September 23 1974   onley

Coburg Island, Baffin Island
PENCIL DRAWING, 1974

Without the support of Prime Minister Pierre Trudeau, it is doubtful that my first voyage into the High Arctic would have taken place. For this I owe him my deepest gratitude. I am also grateful to Capt. Paul Fournier and the officers and crew of the CCGS *Louis S. St. Laurent,* who were most understanding of my purposes. Especial thanks go to the ship's carpenter who in his spare time made me a drawing board on which to paint my first Arctic watercolours.

Many old friends and not a few strangers assisted me greatly on my 1975 solo flight into the Arctic. Particularly, I would like to thank weatherman David Petznick for his hospitality at Bissett, Manitoba; the operator of the fishing camp at Sabourin Lake, Ontario, and the Beech 18 pilot there who put me back on course. More thanks go to good friend sculptor/pilot Robert Murray and his wife Cintra for their en route hospitality and support; also to Montreal architect Jacques Morin and Suzy Morin for a fine meal and comfortable lodgings given an unexpected guest; and to the fishermen at Sept-Îles, who fed me fresh trout while I waited for the fog to dissipate. Above all, I extend my gratitude to master lithographer Wally Brannen and Terry Ryan, art director of the West Baffin Eskimo Co-op, for their invitation to work with them. Wally and his wife Tessa made my stay on Baffin Island an event of a lifetime. Heartfelt thanks, too, to Koagak, my patient translator and guide, and to the Inuit artists of Cape Dorset for making me welcome. Last but not least, my thanks to the RCMP for monitoring my flight across the Arctic.

For my third Arctic trip I am deeply indebted to the several Federal ministers for their confidence in Claude Péloquin's and my ability to—in the words of Joe Clark—"give expression to a vital aspect of our national character." My appreciation extends to Canadian Coast Guard Northern, especially to Capt. Claude Guimont, his officers and crew; the atmosphere of co-operation aboard the *Des Groseilliers* was inspiring.

A round of thanks goes to my typist Elizabeth Friesen for her patience and uncanny ability to decipher my uncial script. My world is divided into two: those who can read my handwriting and those who cannot. I was fortunate in finding Liz.

Thanks also to my editor Marilyn Sacks who approached my manuscript with a keen interest in Arctic history and with sensitivity towards my observations.

To allay some of the reader's confusion with the seeming inconsistency of metric and non-metric terms in this book, distance on the water and in the air is shown in nautical miles (in the flight section, simply miles); height from a plane is shown in feet. Sightings and other measurements have been computed metrically in keeping with current usage.

Cape Sherard, Devon Island
WATERCOLOUR, 1974

The uncontrollable hazards of watercolour make it an ideal medium for painting in the Arctic—a medium demanding confidence and courage, a medium as capricious as the sea itself. Water is essential to watercolour, and the wetness of the medium contains all the fateful connotations of voyaging in the Arctic.

The watercolours from my 1974 voyage aboard the CCGS *Louis S. St. Laurent* and on my 1975 flight to Baffin Island were done on a French cotton rag paper, BFK Rives and Johannot, which is made by a small French mill. It is similar to Arches, another paper I have used extensively. I have recently switched to T. H. Saunders, an English paper, which I used exclusively on my 1986 voyage aboard the CCGS *Des Groseilliers.* Both papers are lightly sized and totally unforgiving, like Japanese or Chinese papers. The watercolour sinks partially into the surface, making it permanent once it is dry. But the T. H. Saunders paper, unlike any other I have used, does not dry lighter than when first painted or fade as it dries in the sun. Colour strength and tone are retained creating a rich and sensuous watercolour. The weight of paper I prefer is 140 pound, just heavy enough not to require stretching.

I paint directly in response to what is before me, neither outlining nor drawing in pencil beforehand—that for me would be to paint by numbers, the finished painting decided long before completion. I prefer to leave all my options open and not know what the finished work will look like: to be in a position of constantly making decisions from stroke to stroke and even in mid-stroke; to keep the whole work moving and speaking to me until that point when the watercolour says, "I am finished." Painting in watercolour is like the course of life itself, full of disappointments, small successes, and, once in a while, the surprise of a totally unexpected breakthrough. Then it is like Zen, or sex; it's the greatest feeling on earth. I live for those rare times when it all comes together, and for a brief moment I can do no wrong—the watercolour painting itself and I only the observer, along for the ride.

Twenty years ago I designed for myself a watercolour box that could carry fifty sheets of paper, a complete palette of large No. 5 (14 ml) tubes of Windsor and Newton watercolours, a large Chinese goat hair brush, and a collapsible Japanese water container. One half of the 40cm by 40cm box contains three mixing trays and a sliding lid compartment for watercolour tubes. The other half contains my paper cut to 30cm by 38cm, and another long compartment to carry extra tubes of watercolours for longer voyages, in addition to rolls of Scotch tape for taping my watercolour paper to the box lid, which serves as a drawing board. My present box is birch wood, one of several I have made over the years, as they wear out from heavy use and rough treatment in travel. (One was once completely smashed in an airplane crash.) But when my present one wears out, I will not have to make another by hand; my design is now being manufactured by Opus Framers Ltd. of Vancouver, and improvements include a better mixing tray, storage compartments and hardware.

September 25

As we entered Smith Sound, between Cape Isabella and Cape Alexander "the north pillars of Hercules" we met with swell of ice, much of it multiyear and up to ten feet thick. All night the ship lurched and ground through the ice, stopping at times to backup and ram the old ice, and on occasion running full speed up on to the ice and sliding back down with the ships propellers still driving at full forward. It was like being in an earth-quake with no relief, all night. It was frightening, I expected the Louis to be holed any time, being constantly thrown thrown sideways into the sharp ice. I was not able to sleep, so got out of my bunk at 5:00 am before I was thrown out! We had almost arrived at our destination, we could not have been far from the North Water project, camp all night became a flare was sighted at midnight going up from Cape Herschel. Capt. Fournier ran her into the ice four mile distant from Pim Island*. As soon as it was light enough our helicopter got to work evacuating the four men, their belonging and most of the camp. It took until mid-afternoon. It was cold 16°F and a 40 MPH wind blew steady down off Leffort glacier. I spent the day in the crews-nest painting the Cape, historic Pim Island and the wind swept lenticular clouds nipping up over the Leffort glacier. The steel floor of the crewsnest hangs out into the wind and is very cold, I have to wear heavy lined boots to keep my feet warm. Today, I accidently dropped my wet watercolour brush on the deck and it instantly froze to the plate steel. I was only able to free it after sacrificing a few hairs. I was able to do four watercolours. It was among some the most paintable country so far.

These waters are inexorably linked with efforts to reach the North Pole. The name of every bay, Cape, Sound and fiord is associated with acheivment and tragedy. Charles Francis Hall died up here, later his ship Polaris was to be holed and sank in ice a short distance south of our location, 19 of his crew were to drift on an ice floe from October 15 1872 to April 30 of the following year and cover a distance of 1300 miles before being saved off Grady Harbour, Labrador. Major Greely and his

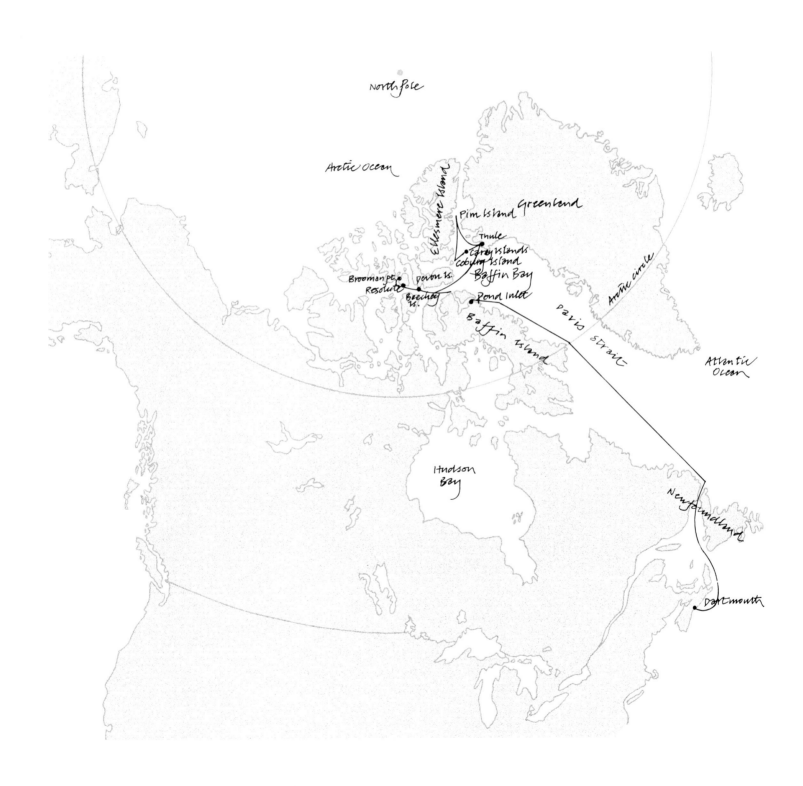

North Pole

Arctic Ocean

Ellesmere Island

Greenland

Pim Island

Thule

Grey Islands

Coburg Island

Baffin Bay

Brooman Pt.
Resolute

Devon Is.

Beechey Is.

Pond Inlet

Baffin Island

Davis Strait

Arctic Circle

Atlantic Ocean

Hudson Bay

Newfoundland

Dartmouth

Navy Board Inlet
WATERCOLOUR, SEPT. 10, 1974

Aktinea Glacier, Bylot Island
WATERCOLOUR, SEPT. 10, 1974

Passing Iceberg
OIL, 1975

SEPTEMBER 8 *Lat.69°40'N Long.64°40'W*

We received a message from the *Labrador* in the night. She is coming out of Jones Sound, and her captain suggests we rendezvous at Eclipse Sound near Pond Inlet. If we arrive tomorrow morning I should be able to do some painting in Pond Inlet.

I had a good day of painting at Cape Dyer. We are following the coast dotted with lonely bergs; by nightfall we are off Cape Christian. It is cold, and black snow clouds are gathering over the land. The bergs are a ghostly pale green in the black water. A school of killer whales go by at 1700 hours. Two of them break off and come over to investigate us.

SEPTEMBER 9 *Lat.71°30'N Long.70°00'W*

By 0800 hours we are off Cape Adair. The *Labrador* is now in Pond Inlet. It is overcast, temperature 10°C and visibility 32 kilometres to the cape. Lots of big bergs are coming down the coast. The sea is so smooth that it feels as if we are riding at dock; not even a swell! I set up my drawing board in the afternoon and do three watercolours of the Baffin Island coast. My studio is the crow's nest, 30 metres above the waterline. I enter it by climbing the inside of the steel mast from the wheelhouse. The crow's nest was designed for operating the ship in the ice from a vantage point but has never been used because few captains of the fleet can fit inside the mast. Also, by law the captain must be in the wheelhouse when the ship is moving in ice. It is 2.5 metres square and glassed in all around, with a spot to jam my drawing board over the electric heater. My watercolours will dry as quickly as I can paint them, and the view is unobstructed. Earlier, I commissioned the "chippy" to make me a drawing board small enough so that I can haul it up to my studio by rope. I have also hauled up a high stool and a gallon of pure icewater to paint with.

We come in progressively closer to shore as we approach Pond Inlet. The landscape is very smooth and sculptured, as though a Henry Moore had shaped it. The mountains are rounded; they flow down into glacier valleys, which in turn wind sinuously to the sea where the bergs break off like glass into the strait.

The days are getting longer as we proceed north. It is now 2300 hours and I have just taken some photographs as we enter Pond Inlet. By 0300 hours tomorrow, there will be enough light to read by. There are only about three hours of actual dark, making it possible for me to paint until quite late.

Cape Searle, Baffin Island
WATERCOLOUR, SEPT. 7, 1974

Magda Plateau, Baffin Island
WATERCOLOUR, SEPT. 10, 1974

Kekertuk, Baffin Island
WATERCOLOUR, SEPT. 7, 1974

Point Thule, Bylot Island
WATERCOLOUR, SEPT. 10, 1974

SEPTEMBER 10   *Lat. 78°45'N Long. 78°00'W*

In the morning at 0900 hours we rendezvous with the *Labrador* in Eclipse Sound and spend two hours transferring thirteen coast guard cadets by helicopter to our ship. Earlier, at about 0800 hours, we went over to Pond Inlet to pick up Dr. Maurice Haycock, a retired mineralogist-geologist who will be joining the ship for the remainder of the arctic voyage. He first came to the Arctic in 1926 for a year of geological and geographical exploration in Cumberland Sound. He met A.Y. Jackson, and his travelling companion Sir Frederick Banting, for the first time when their ship stopped at Pangnirtung. Maurice began to paint in the mid-thirties and soon renewed his friendship with Jackson. For many years thereafter they painted together all over Canada and in the sub-arctic Barren Lands. Maurice has since travelled over 480 000 kilometres, mostly in the High Arctic, recording the northern landscapes in his paintings. He and Jackson had flown with our helicopter pilot Blackie years before in the Western Arctic. When Maurice comes on board he is bearing gifts—22 kilograms of arctic char for the ship's larder.

I spend the rest of the morning and all afternoon in my crow's nest studio as we sail out of Eclipse Sound and Navy Board Inlet to Lancaster Sound. It has been the most successful day's painting to date. I have completed twelve watercolours—of bergs, glaciers, mountains and low cloud. For most of the day the ship was envelopped in thick fog, but up in the crow's nest I was out of it, enjoying endless views of Bylot Island and Borden Peninsula.

It is now 2230 hours and still light as we head out into Lancaster Sound across the point where the men of Sir James Ross's expedition were rescued in 1835 by the whaler *Isabella*. They had spent four years in the Arctic, their ship imprisoned by ice, and were making a desperate attempt to escape in long boats when by chance they were spotted off the end of Navy Board Inlet.

From here we head west to Resolute, still in calm, ice-free water. About every hour we steer around a big berg drifting towards us and down the inlet.

SEPTEMBER 11   *Lat. 74°20'N Long. 90°00'W*

By 0800 hours we are off Prince Leopold Island heading west in Lancaster Sound in heavy fog and snow. By noon it clears, and I am able to do two watercolours from the crow's nest: one of the island, still in sight astern of us, and one of Cape Hurd eight kilometres to the north. By 1500 hours we heave to off Beechey Island and go ashore in the helicopter: Dr. Haycock, Dr. Herman Miller (the ship's doctor), Captain Fournier, Chief Engineer Carlson, Maurice and myself. While I am waiting for the helicopter to make a second trip, I sight a cairn on top of the high south cliff of Beechey Island. This turns out to be the one erected by Sir John Franklin in 1845–46 when he and his men wintered there. The Franklin party vanished without a trace two years later, launching a series of searches that has never completely ceased. It was this cairn that Captain Ommanney, commanding the *Assistance*, sighted in his search for Franklin in 1850.

The searchers found evidence of white man's wintering, but no definite proof that it had been the Franklin party, until three graves were discovered about a kilometre to the west of the main camp. The inscription on these graves gave the first clue. They were men from the *Erebus* and the *Terror*, Franklin's ships. I visited these graves, and the painted inscriptions on the wooden gravemarkers are still clear and readable after more than a century.

Graves, Beechey Island
Franklin Expedition, 1845
WATERCOLOUR, SEPT. 11, 1974

A small nineteenth-century sailing vessel, the *Mary*, was left in case the party returned; all that remains is the mast, which stands in the shale pointing defiantly north, and one side of the ship's hull and a few planks lying scattered below at the shoreline. When A. Y. Jackson painted her in 1927, a few of her ribs were still standing. Apart from the little schooner, Jackson found the place "from an artist's point of view... a total loss. There was nothing to paint, the water was muddy, and we could barely see through fog." Some wooden posts and one wall of Northumberland House, built by Sir Edward Belcher in 1854, still stand as well as some stone walls behind which I saw scattered pieces of Welsh coal. The whole site is strewn with barrel staves and large tin cans. A two-metre cross has been laid out on the ground fashioned from these 129-year-old cans. There is a cairn alongside Sir Edward's monument to Franklin; a glass bottle beneath it contains messages from people who have braved it to this spot in the intervening years. I leave my own message in an Edgeworth tobacco tin and place it with the bottle beneath the cairn. History is frozen here. The remains of the epic voyages have become part of a void suspended in time.

The ship is waiting, and we have only an hour at Franklin's winter camp. Maurice, who is making a record of historic sites of arctic explorers, tells me today of his find of last month. Capt. William Penny believed that Franklin went north up Wellington Channel towards the open Polar Sea. Penny wintered at the south end of Cornwallis Island in 1851 and made sledging trips north along Wellington Channel. At the north end of Cornwallis Island he met with open water across which he sighted Baillie Island, so he sent back to his ship for a long boat to get across the narrow stretch of water. This boat was later abandoned, on a beach he called Abandon Bay. Maurice heard that this boat was still there, so he chartered an airplane and flew up. Sure enough, there it was, just as Captain Penny had left it over a century before. The Arctic protects frail evidence for hundreds of years. The only threat to such things of historical importance is man. Quite possibly hunters will come along soon and pepper Penny's boat with bullet holes just as was done to the objects found at Adolphus Greely's 1883 camp at Fort Conger on Ellesmere Island.

I was told of the find of a hand-tooled brass instrument for making pendulum observations set up and used for target practice. The Franklin Probe, a twelve-man team, was camped at Beechey Island this summer. They painted the wooden grave markers white, a most insensitive act bordering on vandalism. They might better have used a transparent penetrating wood preservative as we do with our old west coast totem poles.

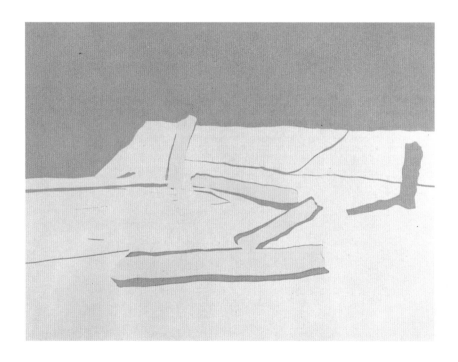

Winter Shore
SERIGRAPH, 1978

Beechey Island
WATERCOLOUR, SEPT. 17, 1974

Iceberg, Eclipse Sound
OIL, 1975

Glacial Boulder
OIL, 1976

Cape Hurd, Parry Channel
WATERCOLOUR, SEPT. 11, 1974

SEPTEMBER 14

When one first sees this land, the thought is that it could not possibly support any life. This is our second day anchored in Pullen Strait, and life is beginning to appear around us. A polar bear with two cubs come out on the ice and play all morning; two seals keep a safe distance on a small floe. I imagine the water to be full of fish. A few days ago when we were approaching Eclipse Sound, the men on the Labrador caught 45 kilograms of arctic char while waiting for us to rendezvous with them.

The weather, clouds and light are constantly changing. I see cloud shadows, patterns in the water and on the hills, and by the time I have run up to my studio, all has changed. Often I just sit in the crow's nest hour after hour and watch it all go by. Part of the ship's mission is to spot and count whales. I am often the first to see them as a result of my vigil. The captain has given me a chart so I can identify them from the shape of their spouts as they blow; I then count them and enter it on a form.

I had no idea that there would be so much colour in the Arctic—not vivid colour but pale, gentle and ever-changing. I have discovered that it is useless to form impressions of places by the descriptions of others: world as is and world as described are two different places. I can understand why explorers returned to the Arctic time after time, as if it were in their blood. This land at times is capable of producing in one an elevated and expanded state of being. On the one hand it is awful and solemn, and on the other it evokes a kind of rapture which must have made those earlier explorers sublimely unconscious of the dangers they faced. So they pushed on in their wooden sailing ships, their captains filled with a blissful superiority born of ignorance, like Robert M'Clure who won a prize of ten thousand pounds for discovering the Northwest Passage, but had to abandon his ship *Investigator* as did his rescuers captains Austin and M'Clintock, who also later abandoned their ships *Intrepid* and *Resolute* about 140 kilometres southwest of this spot in Viscount Melville Sound. In the end, exploring was an addiction, like looking up strange, unfamiliar words in the dictionary for where they may lead.

Every corner we turn reveals different shapes, colours and sights; yet even when you stay in one place, the landscape will change before your eyes. The low cloud drifts across a nearby hill; it lets sun through then shuts it out changing the hill from heavy lamp black to light white. The flight engineer notices it and says, "Geez! Look at that hill; looks like it is floating in the sky!" (The Inuk says, "The land is coming up for air.") "I've been coming up here for years, and it's one hell of a strange place!" Maurice Haycock, who has arctic fever if anyone does, says to me as I lean on the ship's rail and stare into space. "Some country, eh?" A Canadian understatement!

The surveyors have their survey boat *Widgeon* over the side and are working from morning until night, filling in the blank white areas at the top of the map. They have discovered two small islands previously uncharted,

Glacial Boulder/Western Suite
SERIGRAPH, 1980

which now have to be named and given a reality. Ice and land merge making it difficult to tell which is which. Our two new islands were passed over by previous cartographers as being ice hummocks—great blocks of ice thrown up in confusion, like a Cubist's dream. But beneath the blocks lay smooth little islands six metres high. Arctic charts are not as complete or as accurate as navigators would like. While sailing the east coast of Baffin Island, north of Cape Dyer, our navigator changed to the next chart north and found us to be ten nautical miles west of our course; all night we had steamed that much closer to land than we had thought we were. Fortunately we were twice that distance offshore. I was on the bridge when this was brought to Captain Fournier's attention. He became very agitated and paced up and down. The navigator said, "Shall I set a new course for Pond Inlet, sir?" The captain said, "Put me on my original course." So we sailed due east for an hour to get back on our track. Whether he was exercising a captain's right to be cussed, or he had good reason to stay well offshore, who knows? I left the bridge quietly.

Glacier, Navy Board Inlet
OIL, 1975

SEPTEMBER 15

The ship is steaming back and forth in the head of McDougall Sound taking soundings along parallel lines two cables wide. It's a moody day with very dramatic skies playing light and colour changes across the smooth water. I spend part of the morning and afternoon in the crow's nest painting and watching. I do five watercolours, including one of newly discovered Tooke Island which looks more like a drifting hummock of ice than land. While we were steaming along at 7 knots, taking soundings, suddenly the water depth went from 104 fathoms to 2 fathoms. We were coming up fast on a shoal in the middle of the channel. The ship was thrown into reverse and everything not tied down went flying. I'm told these shoals are everywhere in the Arctic, particularly in the Beaufort Sea and Western Arctic. Where such pingos come up to within a few metres of the water's surface on proposed oil tanker routes, they constitute little hidden disasters.

Ice-edge, Riddle Point, Intrepid Passage
WATERCOLOUR, SEPT. 13, 1974

SEPTEMBER 16

After the hydrographers have finished their day of surveying and the heli-copter is free, Maurice Haycock, Dr. Miller, and I fly over to Brooman Point on the east coast of Bathurst Island on Crozier Strait, where there are the remains of a Thule culture settlement. The stone and shale houses were built 2.5 to 3.5 metres round, partly below ground and partly above. The roof members were fashioned from large whalebones over which sealskins were once stretched; moss would have been placed on top to prevent the skins from drying out. After many hundreds, perhaps thousands, of years, this settlement is amazingly intact. The great whalebones point up to the sky, radiating out from the centre of the circles of stone and earth, lying just where they collapsed. There are maybe twenty to thirty dwellings along each shore and out to the point of the peninsula. As we descend in the helicopter at the site, a white fox runs out from under us, and then in his confusion doubles back under and between our skids as we land. He takes off in a straight line as soon as we get out. I see fresh polar bear tracks in the snow. Since the helicopter is to leave us there, I ask the pilot for his flare gun to ward off any bears that might come snooping around. It is a beautiful evening but a little too cold to paint out-of-doors; watercolours freeze at 0°C. I take about three rolls of black-and-white film and fifteen polaroid shots. I pick up a big lichen-encrusted whale vertebra, which Maurice Haycock brings back to the ship for carbon 14 dating. At midnight, when we return to the ship, she is already moving out for Resolute Bay.

Site of Thule Culture dwellings, Brooman Point

Whale Bone, Thule Site,
Brooman Point
OIL, 1975

SEPTEMBER 17   *Lat. 74°40'N Long. 95°20'W*

By 0800 hours we are steaming off Resolute, in Resolute Passage. I spend the morning in the crow's nest and later do a painting of Cape Dungeness at the entrance of Wellington Channel as we go slowly by. Our destination is now Thule, Greenland, about fifty hours' sailing time along the south shore of Devon Island to Baffin Bay. It has started snowing. I paint in my studio all afternoon and into the evening. We sail continuously in and out of snow squalls which produce an ever-changing display of clouds, lights and shadows across the high cliffs of South Devon Island. There is a sharp, brittle quality to the landscape, making it ideally suited to watercolour paints. The complex arrangements of shapes, lights, shadows and colours have to be laid down as quickly as the compositions appear in the eye and mind. I do ten watercolours today, including two of bleak Beechey Island as we returned past it, my Chinese goat hair brush, French handmade papers and English watercolours all coming together in the crow's nest of a Canadian icebreaker to create some of the best work I have done in the medium. Time stops as I move silently and with serenity of mind and body through dissolving clouds. If only I could stay longer. But the season is late, and already new ice —delicate, transparent grease ice—is forming in our path. Soon it will be impassable, and not even our powerful ship will be able to budge out of it.

Old Ice, Cornwallis Island
WATERCOLOUR, SEPT. 15, 1974

Time is now the enemy; we are to be the last ship to return from the Arctic, as we were the last to arrive here. The *Labrador* must be almost home by now, and the *MacDonald* is leaving Resolute for home today, while we head north and into the heavy ice that grows thicker year after year. There are fewer birds to follow us now, only the snow-white little ivory gull and the occasional fulmar gliding across the surface film of new ice.

I watch Beechey Island slip away as we sail east into Lancaster Sound, and think of what I felt when I was there a few short days ago, of the mixed feelings I had then and now—of the beauty of solitary places and how I am drawn to them. But Beechey is also a frightening place, guarding the great Franklin mystery. The silence is deafening. The spirits of the dead are there, prisoners forever in the ice. Men cannot die in agony and not leave a trace! There is a grave of the young officer, John Torrington, his spirit doomed to live out eternity in the frozen shale.

Glacier, Maxwell Bay, Barrow Strait
WATERCOLOUR, SEPT. 17, 1974

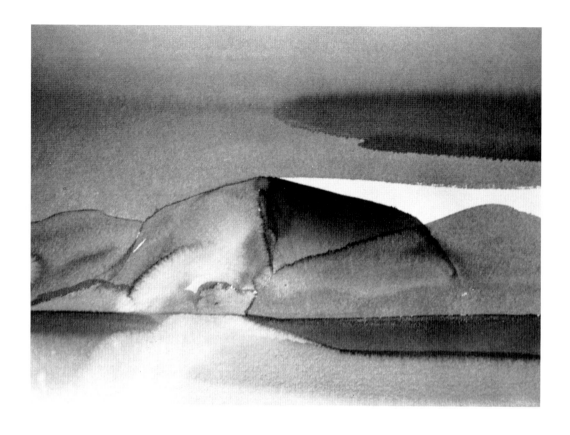

*Cape William Herschel,
Lancaster Sound*
WATERCOLOUR, SEPT. 17, 1974

*Iceberg off Saunders Island,
Wolstenholme Fiord, Greenland*
WATERCOLOUR, SEPT. 19, 1974

Greenland
SERIGRAPH, 1978

SEPTEMBER 18 *Lat. 74°30'N Long. 80°00'W*

As the sun rose this morning we were off Cape Sherard. It took from 0900 hours to 1500 hours to pass the Cunningham Mountains on Devon Island, and I did ten watercolours in that time. There is a great quantity of heavy drifting ice at the entrance to Lancaster Sound, which comes down from Smith Sound. The ice observer went off ahead in the helicopter and counted fifty-three bergs around Cape Sherard. We passed one berg that looked very close but was actually ten kilometres away. The navigator measured the height with the sextant and found it to be 60 metres high and a quarter of a kilometre long. It had smooth vertical sides and a saw-toothed mountain top. A dazzlingly bright sun lit up the ice and mountains of Devon Island.

One of the first impressions one gets of the High Arctic is its immensity. In a land without harbours, we sail to within safe distance of land and take the helicopter ashore. We appear to be very close, as we did at Beechey Island, and heave to under Devon's east wall which rises 180 metres to its tabletop. When we land on shore and look back for the ship, our *Louis*, the largest conventional icebreaker in the world, appears as only a little red-and-white dot and a puff of smoke. The scale is hard to grasp until one spots a building or a village like Pond Inlet. I have difficulty at first locating it without my field glasses even though we are only three kilometres distant. It looks like a scattering of tiny pebbles along the edge of the water; I would never have seen it had it not been pointed out. The scale of the land is out of all proportion to its inhabitants.

Cape Sherard slipped over the horizon behind us at 2000 hours. We will spend all tonight and tomorrow until 1700 hours reaching Thule, across Baffin Bay.

Beechey Island

Cape Sherard, Devon Island
WATERCOLOUR, SEPT. 18, 1974

Glacier, Cunningham Mts., Devon Island
WATERCOLOUR, SEPT. 18, 1974

Iceberg, Baffin Bay/Arctic Suite
SERIGRAPH, 1989

SEPTEMBER 19 *Lat. 76°00'N Long. 71°00'W*

When I awake this morning, we are already among the massive flow of
icebergs that drift down the Greenland coast to the Atlantic. The ship has
slowed down to manoeuvre around these giants slipping down the sides of
the earth. The sea is lake calm. I look through a glass-bottomed bucket at
the permanent world frozen into majestic forms. Stillness rests like light on
the great expanse of Baffin Bay. Occasionally a piece from a berg hits the bow,
sending shudders throughout the ship with the sound of a great temple gong.

The vast expanse of icebergs, changing shapes as we glide between them,
is too much for the mind and eye to take in at one time. I can paint only selec-
ted fragments of what lies before me.

After entering the fiord between Wolstenholme and Cape Athol, I settle
down to painting: the red stratified sedimentary rock of the islands is topped
with pink algae-coloured snows; ridged cliffs, like crumpled red paper, are
arranged as accidentally as clouds, and grounded icebergs lie at their feet.
I do three watercolours before we dock at Thule.

We picked up Roger Braithwaite, Atsumu Ohmura and Karl Schroff of the
North Water Project along with their equipment. The American Air Force
Base is a collection of aluminum boxes in long depressing rows connected by
umbilical cords of heating pipes, waste pipes and electrical conduits. The
personnel are hermetically sealed off from the beautiful harsh land of rock
and unending ice cap which loom above. Across the bay from the dock lies
the native village, at the foot of black tabletop Dundas Mountain. The Inuit
are very friendly. The men, in chaplike pants made from polar bear skins,
look like scaled-down cowboys. They are hardy people to have lived for
centuries beyond the tree line, beyond the cropline, in a land covered 90 per
cent by ice more than 1600 metres deep. The American explorer Charles
Francis Hall called them "a link between Saxons and seals—hybrids, putting
the seals' bodies into their own and then en-casing their skin in the seals.'"
At the edge of the village I can see the little white house of the Danish
explorer Knud Rasmussen, as it was when he occupied it except now it has
electricity—a convenience he never enjoyed. The house was built earlier in
this century; it was the place from which he carried out a series of Thule
expeditions, seven in all, starting in 1912, covering a vast terrain by dog team
and sled which included traversing the Northwest Passage by land.

SEPTEMBER 20 *Lat. 76°32'N Long. 68°50'W*

We leave Thule at 0800 hours and sail down Wolstenholme Fiord heading
northwest out into Baffin Bay, once more amongst ghostly bergs on their
silent way to haunt the North Atlantic. Our destination is Cape Herschel.
We are taking the historic route of William Baffin, who, on his voyage of 1616,
discovered the open North Water, an area of the sea approximately the size of
Switzerland, which never freezes. We sail again under clear skies and calm
water until we round Høkluyt Island and meet with a head-on gale pushing
mountainous waves. These winds come down the fiords of the Greenland ice

cap dead ahead of us, just as they met Baffin in his tiny ship Discovery. As he approached Steensby Land off Cape Leiningen, a severe storm blew. He took refuge in the lee of Høkluyt Island, which "lyeth between two great Sounds, the one Whale Sound... and the other Sir Thomas Smith's Sound; this last runneth to the North of 78°, and is admirable in one respect, because in it is the greatest variation of the compasse of the world known; for by divers good observations I found it to be above five points, or fifty-six degrees varied to the westward." We are to arrive at Sir Thomas Smith's Sound by 2000 hours where the scientists of the North Water Project are to take deep water samples to discover the origin of these waters. We carry on to Cape Herschel to evacuate the Project's camp. The men have been here for three years.

The coastline of Greenland north of Thule is powerful. It has great variety, rugged capes and deep fiords ending in sharp white glaciers. The rock everywhere is deep red with purple shadows. The eroded gullies down the face of every cliff look as though sharp fingers had been drawn down through soft red clay before it had frozen. But against the blue-black waters, the land looks amazingly soft, topped with pink snows, joining almost imperceptibly with the pink sky. I do seven watercolours in the crow's nest until the sea picks up violently. It is like being at the top of a tall, thin tree in a hurricane. I empathize with Turner who had himself bound to the mast of a ship in a storm to get the feel of it.

SEPTEMBER 21   *Lat. 78°15'N Long. 74°00'W*

As we enter Smith Sound, between Cape Isabella and Cape Alexander— named by Capt. John Ross in 1818 after the ships under his command and referred to by him as "the north pillars of Hercules"—we meet with a wall of ice, much of it multiyear and up to three metres thick. All night the ship lurches and grinds through it, stopping at times to back up and ram the old ice, and on occasion to run full speed up onto it and slide back down with the ship's propellers still driving full forward. It is frightening, like being in a continuing earthquake. I expect the *Louis* to be holed any time. Unable to sleep, I get out of my bunk at 0500 hours before being thrown out.

Glacier, Cape Herschel, Smith Sound
WATERCOLOUR, SEPT. 21, 1974

In 1927 when the old steamship *Beothic,* carrying A.Y. Jackson and his friend Dr. Banting, pushed her way into these waters off Pim Island and Bache Peninsula it was indeed hazardous. Captain Falke's hair must have turned grey during these voyages to supply Canada's most northerly RCMP station. Because of the risk, the RCMP post was later abandoned. The ice-carrying waters in this area move as fast as a river and crushed many ships.

We have almost arrived at our destination. We cannot have been far from the North Water Project camp all night, because a flare was sighted from the bridge at midnight going up from Cape Herschel. Captain Fournier has run the *Louis* into the ice six kilometres distant from Pim Island. Lat. 78°40' is our farthest penetration north. Fritz Müller told me he had landed at Pim Island three years earlier in search of a site for the North Water Project. He found what looked like an ideal site, except for a number of graves of white men who had been buried aboveground under piles of stones. They were well preserved, some in sailcloth shrouds and nineteenth-century dress. The foxes and bears had got at some of the bodies beneath the stones, as skulls lay strewn around. He discovered also a large wood and coal-burning cast-iron stove of the kind used in nineteenth-century sailing ships. The site depressed him so much that he eventually located his camp at Cape Herschel, a few kilometres to the south. There were also practical considerations for this change of location: the bodies could have contaminated a nearby small lake. The graves could not have been those of the Greely expedition, because all the men who died at that time were taken out. Maurice Haycock, the historian of our group, could not shed any light on this discovery.

As soon as it is light enough, our helicopter begins evacuating the four men, their belongings, and most of the camp. It takes until mid-afternoon. It is cold (-4°C) with a 65-kph wind blowing steadily off Leffert Glacier. I spend the day in the crow's nest painting the cape, historic Pim Island, and the windswept lenticular clouds whipping up over the glacier. The steel floor of the crow's nest hangs out into the wind and is very cold. Even my heavy, lined boots barely keep my feet warm. When I accidentally drop my wet watercolour brush on the deck, it instantly freezes to the plate steel. I am able to free it only after sacrificing some hairs. This is some of the most paintable country so far, and I am able to do four watercolours.

These waters are inexorably linked with efforts to reach the North Pole. The name of every bay, cape, sound and fiord is associated with achievement and tragedy. Charles Francis Hall died here; later his ship, *Polaris*, was holed and sank in ice a short distance south of our location. Nineteen of his crew drifted on an ice floe from October 15, 1872, to April 30 of the following year and covered a distance of 2100 kilometres before being saved off Grady Harbour, Labrador. The American Major Adolphus Greely and a party of men slowly starved while waiting for a relief ship; only seven of the original expedition of twenty-five survived. Greely's "Starvation Camp" sits four nautical miles off our bow, its top obscured from sight by fine, blowing snow.

Cape Abernathy,
Baffin Bay, Greenland
WATERCOLOUR, SEPT. 20, 1974

Ice Floe, Cape Herschel,
Smith Sound
WATERCOLOUR, SEPT. 21, 1974

Dr. Elisha Kent Kane, another American explorer (for whom the Great Basin is named), in an attempt to reach the pole in 1853–55, was forced to winter at Rensselaer Harbour on the Greenland side of Smith Sound just off our stern. His story, like that of Greely later, was filled with tragedy. Robert Peary came this way on his way to the Pole. Knud Rasmussen, whose schooner A. Y. Jackson and Lawren Harris had seen in Robertson Fiord, Greenland, in 1930, had trecked all over the region. From the crow's nest I had a spectacular view of our return through the ice. It was quite a ride; I had to hang on tight until we reached the open waters of Baffin Bay.

Our next stop in the evacuation of the North Water Project is Coburg Island at the entrance to Jones Sound. Our ETA is 0800 hours tomorrow. The days are shortening very fast now. Each day the sun sets perceptibly sooner. The long arctic night begins three weeks from today.

SEPTEMBER 22 *Lat. 75°46'N Long. 79°15'W*

It is a clear, sunny day with visibility unlimited as we enter the ice floes to the north of Coburg Island. But a black cloud hangs over the island, and by the time we reach Cambridge Bay on the south side, the cloud cover spreads out from the islands' mountain peaks and obscures all the southern horizon. The helicopter gets to work immediately on the ship's arrival to evacuate the North Water Project's three scientists and all their equipment. Maurice and I are taken onto the island on the second trip of the helicopter. I can see the weather closing in as our helicopter leaves the ship and I know there is a good possibility that we may not get back today. But I am still eager to see the island. The overcast gives it a mysterious look as though it holds secrets that cannot be seen from the ship. The mountains, steep valleys and glaciers are very inviting. We fly into Cambridge Bay and down a steep-sided valley opening out onto a wide plain that sweeps around a bay about 13 kilometres long. At the south end of this unnamed bay stands the little camp. The helicopter makes two trips with sling cargoes before the ceiling drops down to obscure the approach valley. We are trapped until the weather improves. There are seven of us: Maurice and I, Fritz Müller, and four students from the University of Zürich, all squeezed into a very small cabin. Fortunately, the two beds and a box of sleeping bags still remain. We have food and a stove which takes the chill off the small cabin; our body heat does the rest.

Carey Island

Carey Island evacuation

At night, the wind gets up to 40 knots and the temperature goes down to 18°C. New grease ice streaks across the bay, pale green on the black water; it smooths the waves like oil. The wind, entering through cracks, whirls the fine snow around the cabin and into a great drift behind it. At night it filters in everywhere; as I lie on the floor in my sleeping bag, it sprinkles my face, stinging like salt on an open wound.

SEPTEMBER 23 *Lat. 75°53'N Long. 79°00'W*

When I awake it is strangely still; the wind has died completely away. I dress and go outside while the others sleep on, some on the floor, one under the table, one on a shelf. The snow has drifted around the cabin creating beautifully carved ridges trailing away from the corners. Two little spiral mounds of snow move and out pop two husky dogs.

The bay is the strangest place I have ever seen. Its beauty is almost supernatural. Huge blocks of ice packed closely together float in the bay. The sky is low and black. The ice blocks have a ghostlike green-blue glow, as though lit up from inside. I feel as if I were standing in a great enclosed hall like the Blue Grotto.

I take a number of walks during the day to make notes to draw from in the cabin. It is far too cold to work outside without gloves. One of the huskies keeps me company. The other one has two week-old pups and so stays behind the cabin curled up in the snow with her babies. The dogs were brought over from Greenland to keep the polar bears away from the camp, but they became pets and lost a lot of their natural fighting instinct. They allowed one bear to get to the cabin early in the morning a few days ago. One of the men jumped out of bed and grabbed a gun as the bear smashed in the cabin window; he fired off a shot, creasing the window frame, and the bear took off, leaving the dogs cowering around the other side of the cabin.

Louis breaking ice

During the day I do five drawings on paper I find in the cabin. I am beginning to get into a routine and am getting used to the cold. Another day has passed and still no let-up in the low ceiling and obscured valley to the camp.

Night comes with no sign of our helicopter. We settle in to a good supper including freshly baked bread. Over coffee I listen to tall arctic tales. Dr. Müller tells us how a German weather station was set up in northern Greenland during the second World War, manned by twenty men. The Germans discovered the ski tracks of Danish explorer Lange Koch and tracked him down. Koch held them off singlehandedly until a sledge patrol came along and captured all but two of the Germans, who died in the shooting. Maurice gives us a rundown on the explorers of this area of the Eastern Arctic.

Once we heard a plane and all ran out but discovered that it was the weather-observing Electra on its way to Thule, high above the clouds, droning away from us.

Toni Onley on Carey Island

Grounded iceberg, Coburg Island, September 23 1974

North water project, camp, Coburg Island. September 23 1974

Grounded Iceberg, Coburg Island
PENCIL DRAWING, SEPT. 23,1974

*North Water Project Camp,
Coburg Island*
PENCIL DRAWING, SEPT. 23,1974

piled-upice, coburg Island, September 23 1974   *onley*

SEPTEMBER 24

We are awakened from sleep by the unmistakable chop-chop-chop of our helicopter. We run out in our longjohns, waving and shouting. We knew the *Louis* was dangerously low on fuel and was eating up 30 tonnes a day just waiting to get us off Coburg, but they have not left us as we had feared.

We are back at the ship by 0800 hours, in time for a good breakfast. The helicopter finishes picking up everything at the camp, and by noon we are ready to sail for the Carey Islands. I spend most of the day in my warm crow's nest studio painting the mountains of Coburg and the rock to the southeast of the island called Princess Charlotte Monument. As we sail east, both Maurice and I paint this monument—paintings which we will later exchange.

I was to learn later that the husky dogs were destroyed. There was no alternative; they could not be set loose on the island to breed into a pack. And they could not be taken back to Thule, a foreign country: importation would have involved too much red tape. We could not give them away in Resolute, for Canadian Inuit now use snowmobiles instead of dogs. The Greenland Inuit are the only ones still using dogs extensively, and they would have no use for animals that had been made into pets. As many as five hundred dogs at Jakobhavn, Greenland, are shot every summer by police because they get loose and are very dangerous. Nevertheless, I enjoyed those huskies during my short stay on Coburg, and it took the wind out of me to hear of their end. Shot and left to be eaten by the bears. Nothing can be buried in the Arctic; even humans are food for bears and fox.

Piled-up Ice, Coburg Island
PENCIL DRAWING, SEPT. 23, 1974

Icefloes, Abandoned Bay, Coburg Island, September 23 1974 — *oulen*

*Icefloes, Abandoned Bay,
Coburg Island*
PENCIL DRAWING, SEPT. 23, 1974

SEPTEMBER 25   *Lat. 76°40'N Long. 73°30'W*

Thirty-knot winds, overcast and cold when we arrive at the Carey Islands
early this morning. The Careys are about 30 nautical miles west of Cape
Parry, Greenland, and, like Greenland, belong to Denmark. William Baffin
named them as he sailed past on his return journey aboard the *Discovery* in
1616. The little cluster of five small islands is associated mainly with the
attempts of two young "unknown" explorers from Switzerland, Alfred
Björling and E. G. Kallstenius, to reach the pole in 1892. Their story is told by
Farley Mowat in his book *The Polar Passion*. They put ashore to avail
themselves of an old cache left here by a British Polar expedition, under   Sir
George Nares, sixteen years earlier in 1876. While they were doing this, their
little leaky schooner, named *Ripple*, was driven onto the rocks and
destroyed. (Today, the current is so strong that the Louis has to keep up a good
head of steam to prevent her drifting onto these same rocks.) Björling, his
companion, and the remaining crew of three—one died on Carey for reasons
not explained—set off for the coast of Ellesmere Island in a small boat, a
distance of 80 nautical miles when Greenland was only 30 miles distant.
(The powerful current here may have made that decision for them.) A packet
of four letters left in a cairn on Carey tells of their departure for Cape
Clarence. No trace of the little party or their boat has ever turned up.

There are two men and one woman to be taken off Carey, along with their
equipment. I take the first flight over with Fritz Müller in order to spend the
day there photographing while cargo is being slung over by the helicopter.
The camp is on the main island of the group. The Careys are very rocky
islands; I had to constantly climb up and down over rocks and through snow-
drifts at the bottom of grey rock peaks whose tops were obscured in swirling
cold mists. The coast around the site was a mass of beached icebergs.
I scrambled around the island over rocks bleached with cold into colours
of pale rosey umbers. Once I slipped and shinned myself badly, but my legs
were so frozen with the wind and snow that I didn't feel it, and forgot all
about it until someone later noticed my blood-soaked pants.

The North Water Project camp here is like a well-kept home; the touches of the female member, Anna Marie, are everywhere from lamp shades to a neat, well-organized kitchen. The walls are covered with maps of the area and pictures; and, as at the Coburg Island camp, last year's Christmas decorations still hang from the ceiling. Since it is well above tree line, the group had drawn a Christmas tree on the wall and taped decorations and candies to it. The quote of the year, taped to the wall, read: "The helicopter is coming on Wednesday." These three had not left the island for a year. There was much excitement and laughter, with everyone talking in Swiss-German at the same time. Over hot soup, they all excitedly exchanged news of the last year. As we sat around warm in our company, Fritz looked out the window and said, "It looks like we stay a while." It was snowing hard, and flying visibility was zero. It could have been Coburg Island all over again, but the weather cleared in an hour. Then the wind got up with the sun and blew so hard the helicopter could not leave the deck of the Louis. It seemed as if we might be stranded, but the wind dropped to 35 knots, and we all got to the ship before dark. A black raven, the Arctic's largest "songbird," gave us a send-off from the roof of the abandoned cabin. We will be in Thule again tomorrow at 0800 hours.

That night the northern lights put on a great display like organ pipes. In the Arctic the northern lights surround you. This display coincided with a radio blackout. Fritz Müller tells me it has been his observation that the aurora puts on its biggest display every nine years. A good year was 1962. So was 1971, and supposedly 1980 and 1989 will be too.

SEPTEMBER 27 *Lat. 77°29'N Long. 69°21'W*

We stop at Thule just long enough to drop off Dr. Müller and his fourteen scientists who will fly on to Trenton in a Canadian Armed Forces Hercules this morning. Maurice is also leaving the ship here and going out on the same aircraft.

We sail out again as soon as we have dropped them at the dock, destination Lancaster Sound and Resolute. Our departure once more is through drifting icebergs, all new and different shapes this time. Their colours change from one horizon, where they are grey-blue, to the other horizon, where they are veridian green. They look so fresh, I picture them calving off the 96-kilometre-long Humboldt glacier—a glacier Kane described as "rising in a solid glassy wall three hundred feet above the water, with an unknown unfathomable depth below it—a long ever-shining line." I do three watercolours before lunch at which time we run headlong into a hurricane. It comes on us so suddenly that I am taken by surprise. After nearly a month of continual sailing, with hardly a wave to rock the ship, suddenly we are in 12-metre waves with wind shipping surf from their tops. Great waves crash into our port side rolling the ship over 45°. I rush to my cabin to secure the furniture, books and my cameras.

Iceberg
SERIGRAPH, 1975

	JOURNEY	CREW	RECORD OF TIME				
1. DATE 1975	2. FROM PREVIOUS LINE TO	3. NAMES	4. UP	5. DOWN	6. AIR TIME	FLIGHT TIME	7. TOTAL AIR TIME SINCE MFG.
			BROUGHT FORWARD ➡				
July 1	Gore Bay - Lookout Island, Onley	1130	1230	1:00		160.62
" 2	Lookout Is - Orangeville, Onley	940	1050	1:05		161.79
" "	Orangeville - Toronto Is. Onley	1210	1235	:25		162.24
" "	Toronto Is. - Lookout Is. Onley	1320	1500	1:40		163.85
" 3	Lookout Is Local Toni Onley	955	1005	:10		163.98
" 4	" " Toni Onley	1000	1015	:15		164.25
" "	" Sudbury SPB Toni Onley	1200	1245	:45		164.97
" "	SPB - Sudbury Toni Onley	1300	1310	:10		165.18
" "	Sudbury - Lookout. Toni Onley	1330	1435	1:05		166.15
" 5	Lookout Is. - Orangeville Onley	720	8:15	:55		167.20
" "	Orangeville - Toronto / Onley	1010	1030	:20		167.53
" "	Toronto - Lookout Is. / Onley	1205	1330	1:25		168.89
" 6	Lookout Is. - S. Limestone Is. / Onley	1405	1420	:15		169.33
" "	Limestone - Parry Sound / Onley	1500	1520	:20		169.71
" "	Parry S. Lookout Is. Toni Onley	1600	1620	:20		170.00
" 7	Lookout Is. Local Toni Onley	1510	1520	:10		170.22
" 9	" Bonniechere / Onley	800	920	1:20		171.52
" "	Bonniechere - Carp / Toni Onley	1055	1140	:45		172.27
" "	Carp - Dorval / Toni Onley	1725	1835	1:10		173.37
" 10	Dorval - St. Irénée Toni Onley	1150	1410	2:20		175.73
" 11	St. Irénée L. Pentecôte Toni Onley	1035	1235	2:00		177.64
" "	L. Pentecôte - Sept Iles / Onley	1445	1535	:50		178.35
" "	Sept-Iles - Schefferville / Onley	1620	1900	2:40		180.91
" 14	Schefferville - Fort Chimo / Onley	6:30	910	2:25		183.69
" "	Fort Chimo - Frobisher Bay / Onley	1050	1430	3:40		187.29
" "	Frobisher Bay - Cape Dorset / Onley	1525	1815	2:50		190.11
" 18	Cape Dorset Local / Onley	1450	1520	:30		190.60
" 21	" " " Toni Onley	2300	0040	1:40		192.21
" 26	" " Nottingham Is. / Onley	1240	1350	1:10		193.30
" "	Nottingham Is. - C. Dorset / Onley	1640	1800	1:20		194.68
" 30	C. Dorset Local Toni Onley	2115	2140	:25		195.05
Aug. 1	" " C. James Toni Onley	1100	1145	:45		195.80
" "	C. James, Aberdeen In. Onley	1200	1230	:30		196.70
			TOTAL THIS PAGE				

THE FLIGHT OF THE *NAUYAUYAQ*

*A 10 000-Kilometre Odyssey by Flying Boat
from Vancouver to Cape Dorset*

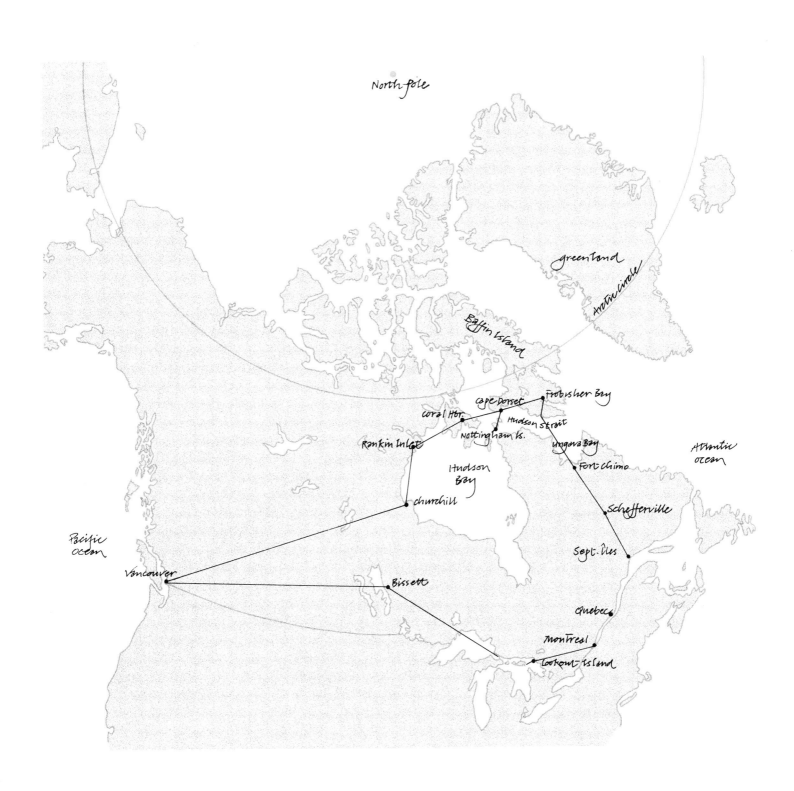

North Pole

Greenland

Arctic Circle

Baffin Island

Frobisher Bay

Cape Dorset

Coral Hbr.

Hudson Strait

Nottingham Is.

Ungava Bay

Rankin Inlet

Fort Chimo

Atlantic Ocean

Hudson Bay

Schefferville

Churchill

Sept-Îles

Pacific Ocean

Vancouver

Bissett

Quebec

Montreal

Lookout Island

For years I had harboured dangerous thoughts of flying my own plane into the Canadian Arctic. (I had had my pilot's licence since 1967.) On cold winter nights I would spread out aeronautical charts on the living room floor in front of a log fire and "fly" over great stretches of featureless landscape, often marked "area of compass unreliability, relief data incomplete." My 1974 sojourn aboard the *Louis S. St. Laurent* only whetted my appetite for such a trip. But to fly over vast reaches of ice-clogged water in my little taildragger Champion Sky-Trac would have been to put eternity beneath my wheels.

Then, during the winter of 1974–75, following up on the enthusiastic response of my friend Robert Murray to his new Lake amphibian flying boat, I acquired a Lake Buccaneer with a turbo-charged engine, which would give me sea level performance up to 20,000 feet—an ideal aircraft for exploring the West Coast and high mountain lakes of British Columbia. It also opened the door to a return to the Arctic, this time as my own navigator.

An invitation from the West Baffin Eskimo Co-operative in Cape Dorset to make a series of lithographs in their print workshop supplied the incentive. Spring 1975 was spent familiarizing myself with the new flying boat and assembling the gear needed to get me to the Eastern Arctic and back.

JUNE 29

One reads of the joys of an early morning departure—of preflighting the aircraft in the wet grass to the sounds of awakening birds, of climbing out into clear, still air as though the plane were on rails. Richard Bach can make it sound very convincing; however, in reality everything conspires to prevent the pilot from getting underway, and my departure today was considerably delayed by an anxious wife whose vivid imagination conjured up all manner of misadventure for me. After promising to call at every stopover, at least until I get into the Arctic, and giving a good-bye hug to my eight-year-old son Jamie, I was off into a mid-morning sun.

JULY 11 *Schefferville Lat.47°35'N Long.70°12'W*

I'm in shape for the flight ahead after a good night's rest. It is 1030 by the time I say all my good-byes and get under way. From the Manicouagan Peninsula, I can see fog on the river up towards Pointe-des-Monts, so I head inland. When I come out at Port Cartier, I meet the fog again. I call Sept-Îles only to hear that they are zero-zero. There is nothing for it but to head inland again and land on one of the long finger lakes running north of my position. I put down on Lac Pentecôte and taxi up to a group of fishermen who are making lunch over an open fire. They invite me to join them. By 1500 hours weather reports on the Sept-Îles beacon call for visual flight rules. I make my way to Sept-Îles, gas up and file a flight plan for Schefferville via the railroad—the iron compass heading straight north. For the first time in my long detour, I feel I am finally on course for the Arctic. The westerly wind increases as I head north, and I land at Schefferville full controls into a 35-knot, 90° crosswind. High winds keep me on the ground for three days in beautiful clear weather. If I had landed at Squaw Lake seaplane base just a kilometre out of town, the crosswind problem could have been eliminated.

JULY 14 *Schefferville Lat.54°48'N Long.66°48'W*

My fourth day in Schefferville. I file a flight plan to Fort Chimo and take off at 0630 hours before the wind gets up. There are 750-metre hills across my route, obscured in cloud, so the safest and best route is northwest—down Otelunk Lake, Chakonipau Lake and along Lac le Moyne to Fort McKenzie (which consists of one log cabin), joining up with the Kaniapskan River and following it to the Kokspak River and on into Fort Chimo. This is a nice, relaxed finger-following flight through magnificent landscape. Small stunted trees persist all the way to Fort Chimo where they stop abruptly, giving way to typical arctic cover of pale green, black and burnt sienna lichen-covered rock. The valleys are alive with the colour of yellow arctic poppies and purple, blue and white flowers which I can't distinguish from the air. The lakes are outlined with pale green water plants.

It is 0900 hours when I approach Fort Chimo high over a herd of musk-ox, remnants of the Ice Age, grazing like cows in a valley below. The rain and clouds are behind me and ahead are clear, bright skies. Ungava Bay stretches away to Cape Hopes Advance; little clouds cap pyramid-shaped hills, 140 miles to the east. I gas up at Fort Chimo and file a flight plan to Frobisher Bay. After checking—full rich, full fine pitch, full throttle—I begin my takeoff, but something is wrong. I am developing only 2300 RPM over 2850 inches manifold pressure, a dangerous combination. With lots of runway, I chop power and taxi back to find my trouble. The propeller pitch control arm has worn off the ball socket and is hanging free. There are no mechanics around so I spend an hour in a cloud of mosquitoes lock-wiring it together. Then off again and up the west coast of Ungava Bay.

Even though the skies are clear, I choose to fly low over the tundra to get the best possible view. The shore of Tiercel Island and Hopes Advance Bay are piled high with great blocks of ice, called "bergy bits." Hoping to find gas in the Inuit hamlet of Bellin, I circle the area but can't find an airstrip, and the bay is rough, so I decide to continue to Frobisher Bay. The black, smooth, shining rock of Cape Hopes Advance passes beneath as I climb to 10,000 feet to pick up the Frobisher Bay beacon. Nearly 100 miles of open water lies ahead, across Hudson Strait to Observation Cove. Ice floes form a solid sheet, completely blocking the strait below. To the west is open water. I can see as far as Wakeham Bay, 140 kilometers away. It was from there that the first ice patrols were flown in 1927 in fragile wood and fabric aircraft with unreliable engines. Meta Incognita Peninsula is covered in cloud, and I can't be sure Frobisher Bay is still clear. Fighting the temptation to continue on top, I descend to 500 feet and fly up Barrier Inlet, following the river to the centre of the peninsula, only to discover that the valleys are blocked off in cloud. A patch of open sky lets me circle up to have another look. The great inlet of Frobisher Bay and its islands are visible ahead; it is all down hill the rest of the way. I am number two to land behind Nordair's DC3 coming in from Cape Dorset, my final destination. There is no sign of the commercial plane and I found out later that it had turned back because of strong crosswinds.

My little Lake parks among the workhorses of the Arctic: DC3s, Skyvans, Twin Otters, Buffaloes and Hercules—not a light plane in sight. I gas up and head for the weather office. There is still good visibility at Cape Dorset, but the ceiling is coming down. I can probably get there if I leave immediately. A heading of 280° true comes out at 329° magnetic, and it is difficult to read the slowly rotating compass. With the help of several landmarks and my directional gyro, I get to Amadjuak, an old Hudson's Bay post last used in 1933. From there I can follow the coast. Frobisher Bay radio calls me to say they don't want to scare me but Cape Dorset is now down to 800 feet. I thank them and say I will carry on. If it gets too bad I will wait it out in one of the inlets. The Cape Dorset non-directional beacon is now coming in strong across the great gulf of Andrew Gordon Bay. I choose to swing around the bay among the islands. The weather is deteriorating. Fog swoops by in wisps, occasionally giving me a glimpse of the next rocky island.

I am flying a few feet off the water now. There are whitecaps and long streaks across my track, indicating a strong breeze of 35 knots. Once in a while I fly over a little white tent, a dark green Montreal canoe pulled up on a rocky beach and a handful of Inuit at their summer camp. They wave and I can see they are shouting. The children run along the rocks as if to keep up with me. The presence of these fishing camps, with men clad in fur parkas ready to greet me if I am forced to land, is comforting. I make note of the time I pass each camp so that I can time myself back if the need arises. The compass indicates a heading almost due north, as the automatic direction finder guides me west to Cape Dorset. Many inukshuit (stone figures) dot this part of the arctic landscape.

I fly low over Foxe Island in Catherine Bay. Just 25 miles east of Cape Dorset, at Enukso Point, stand more than one hundred stone figures, mute guardians of a frigid sea. They are warm comfort to me as man-made objects; people and shelter must be close at hand. Many more of these stone people are visible as I fly low around Andrew Gordon Bay; from headland to headland they guide me to my destination just as they have guided Inuit for centuries.

Finally, out of the fog, rises Kingnuit Hill, the great rocky bluff standing guard over Cape Dorset Bay. I make a steep, low swing over the settlement before climbing to the runway above. By the time I land, a jeep is waiting with two RCMP officers, one white, one Inuk. They help me tie the Lake to 205-litre oil drums and congratulate me on my crosswind landing. The winds are gusting to 45 knots, and mine is the first plane to land in a week. Then my hosts arrive: master lithographer Wallace Brannen and his wife Tessa. I will spend the next month with them, painting out on Foxe Peninsula and making lithographs in the West Baffin Eskimo Co-operative workshop.

Cape Dorset is a unique Inuit settlement, almost exclusively concerned with the production of prints and carvings in stone and ivory. It is the wealthiest of the many Inuit co-operatives across the Arctic. [At that time the average income here was $20,000 per capita, making it the highest in North America, and probably in the world.] Lithography has only been introduced to the Inuit artists in the full professional sense in the past year. Wallace Brannen is a graduate of Tamerand Institute and former head of the Nova Scotia College of Art and Design's litho workshop, where he worked with such American artists as Sol Lewitt and Claes Oldenburg. He came here in 1972 at age twenty-three to set it up and train the Inuit artists in the production of fine litho prints, working with artists like Pudlo, Kingmeata and Peter Pitseolak. Since the major artists of the community are the older men and women, few speak English, so demonstration is the best form of communication.

JULY 15

Wally Brannen and I had previously worked together in Halifax at the college, and he knows he can count on me to settle in and produce. With a few days of glorious weather, I am able to work outdoors on my watercolours, which gives me a feel of the land and images to work with in the litho shop. Just as I complete my outdoor work, the weather closes in, and the cape is shrouded in black arctic fog. The timing must have happened by some divine plan, for now I am able to concentrate on drawing on the large limestones in the workshop. (The limestone comes from Solnhofen, Bavaria; although many substitutes are quarried in various parts of the world, all are inferior to this.)

Cape Dorset

The weather also brings in the Inuit artists from seal hunting and fishing. The little shop is full of activity as we elbow for work space. The air fills with smoke and the gutteral sounds of Inuktitut. At first the Inuit ignore me as I work away in my corner and then, as the drawings come together on the limestones and proofs are pulled, they gather around and talk animately together about them. Eegyvudluk recognizes my drawing of an inukshuk. He pokes me in the ribs with delight and exclaims with gusto, "In-uk-shuk," and we all laugh. The ice is broken. From now on they help me sponge my lithography stones, cut paper to the size required for my work, and look long and considerately at my print as it is peeled from the stone, and I do the same with their work.

Pudlo, who works quietly in the corner with his cigarette and a can of coke (the locals devour 700,000 cans a year), is doing his first lithograph, drawing with a very soft litho crayon. Seeing the fine lines in my drawing on the stone, he comes over and slips the crayon from my hand, checks the number then puts it back into my hand without a smile or expression. He chooses a harder crayon for himself from then on. I often think of this incident when I see Pudlo's finely drawn prints characterized by images of the spirit world.

Much of the drawing and printmaking of the Inuit deals not only with the spirit world but also with the people themselves. Their art is filled with animals, birds and men engaged in the difficult and demanding task of the hunt. When the graphic artist Parr was drawing with great concentration and rapid strokes, he was, I feel, reliving the excitement and challenge of the hunt. So I am not surprised when Eegyvudluk tells my sixteen-year-old interpreter Koagak at the end of a long day in the print studio that he is going out to catch seal this evening. Never having been on an Inuit hunt before, I ask if I can join him and his companions. He is all smiles, meaning yes! I ask how long we will be out and how I should dress. He says, "About two hours and bring a 'parker.'" I wear rubber boots and duffel socks that a local Inuk woman has made for me, but am clearly unprepared for the long cold night even though we have twenty-four hours of daylight at this time of year.

Wallace Brennan, Toni

Kenojuak

Pudlo, Toni

Arctic Fog, Cape Dorset
WATERCOLOUR, JULY 19, 1975

Cape Dorset
WATERCOLOUR, 1975

Whale Bone Cove, Baffin Island
WATERCOLOUR, JULY 16, 1975

JULY 16

We head off into Pudla Inlet and Catherine Bay in Eegyvudluk's Montreal canoe, a long green canvas and wood craft with an outboard motor. When the three men spot a seal, they all stand together in the canoe excitedly firing off round after round from their rifles before the seal can dive. If one bullet finds its mark, we fire up the motor and race over to harpoon it before it sinks from sight. For every one we catch, one sinks below the harpooners' reach. This time of year the seal does not have a lot of fat so will not float as easily as in spring and autumn. When the first seal is hauled aboard, one of the boys whips out a knife and removes an eye then hands it to me, dripping in the palm of his hand. The Inuit consider this a great delicacy. It tastes not unlike a raw, salty egg but with a harder, chewier texture.

After several hours, my feet already numb from the cold bottom of the canoe, one of the boys spots a beluga whale surfacing. In no time, the whale is surrounded by a dozen canoes that seem to appear from nowhere, their occupants all shooting excitedly. The bullets ricochet off the smooth water and whistle over our heads. I dive to the bottom of the canoe and bury myself among the dead seals, sloshing blood, and sea water until it is all over. The whale has escaped. If I was cold before, I now know what it must be like to freeze to death. My companions think I look very funny. They all laugh uncontrollably as we head for home in the early hours of the morning.

Carey Island, Baffin Bay
LITHOGRAPH

Nottingham Island/Cape Dorset Suite
LITHOGRAPH

Whale Bone Cove/Cape Dorset Suite
LITHOGRAPH

JULY 21   *Nottingham Island   Lat.63°20'N   Long.78°00'W*

South from Cape Dorset lie three large islands like giant stepping stones across Hudson Strait. On the south tip of the southernmost island, called Nottingham Island, there is an old abandoned DOT weather station at Port de Boucherville. The Inuit of Cape Dorset bought a number of buildings several years ago for $5,000 with the idea of using them as a summer workshop for their stone carvers and printmakers. The nearby waters abound with walrus and seal, and the lakes on the island are brimming with arctic char. The Co-op art director and manager, Terry Ryan, has not seen the station for some years, and his last voyage to Nottingham, aboard the Co-op's boat, the *Arluk*, almost ended in disaster when her diesel engine broke down leaving him and his companion drifting in Foxe Basin for days in heavy seas. Terry has dug out a couple of old drums of Avgas (which I later learned were eight or nine years old) to fuel the Lake, and he, Wally Brannen and I set out for the island. Icebergs drift down into Hudson Bay as we cross the tundra of Salisbury Island and head for the fiords of Nottingham Island. It is hard to judge the scale of the land when there are no trees or houses or boats. What looks like a gull on a rock sometimes proves to be a polar bear.

The inlet at Port de Boucherville is sheltered and makes a good landing area. I tie the Lake off at an old stone dock and, being cautious, go back to check on her after about twenty minutes. Rocks are growing out of the shallows all around her, so I untie and push the plane into deeper water, a chore I perform three times as the tide races out. Apparently, the tides here are second in the world only to the Bay of Fundy tides.

With one eye on the plane, we quickly explore the buildings of the abandoned weather station. The bunkhouse, with beds made and magazines scattered around, could have been occupied yesterday except that the papers and magazines are thirty-five years old. There are wartime issues of *Life* and *Saturday Evening Post.* The kitchen is also a time capsule, the shelves filled with canned goods whose forty-year-old labels are still familiar to us today. There are even boxes of cornflakes, crisp and ready to eat. All remains as it was left, except for the generating machinery which has been vandalized, maybe by the boys from Sugluk who killed the walruses that lay rotting around the inlet shore. They were intact except for their ivory tusks; for these they had been killed.

Inukshuit, Cape Dorset
WATERCOLOUR, AUGUST 10, 1975

The receding water cuts our stay short, and after a hasty lunch we depart for Cape Dorset, about 40 minutes flying time northeast of us. As we climb effortlessly into the still, cool, clear air I think of Pitseolak, one of the most accomplished of the Cape Dorset graphic artists, who was born on Nottingham Island around 1900. Her parents and three brothers were on their way from Sugluk on the Quebec coast to Cape Dorset in the spring of that year. They camped on Nottingham Island so that Pitseolak could be born. The family did not arrive at Cape Dorset until the following spring. We are now over Salisbury Island, and only twenty minutes from Cape Dorset we can see the great expanse of the Kingait range and the Foxe Peninsula spread out before us as we slowly descend. Soon we will be home to supper and a warm bed.

Rock, Mallik, Cape Dorset
LITHOGRAPH

Mallik/Cape Dorset Suite
LITHOGRAPH

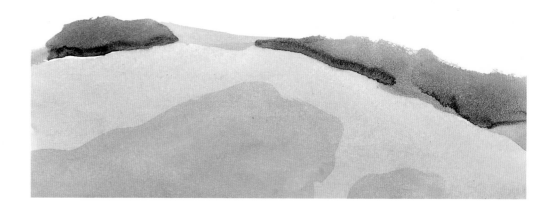

Eskimo Point
OIL, 1976

Nottingham Island
WATERCOLOUR, 1976

Dorset Bay, Baffin Island
WATERCOLOUR, JULY 16, 1975

AUGUST 1 *Cape James Lat.64°22'N Long.74°08'W*

A young man by the name of Okituk comes into Cape Dorset by Montreal canoe. He has travelled 150 nautical miles across Andrew Gordon Bay from Cape James to tell us that the diesel engine in his father's Peterhead boat will not start. Terry Ryan locates the mechanic and we fly off to the rescue. Okituk's father is Kaka, the son of Pitseolak. Kaka, like his father Ashoona, has chosen to live in the old way, in camp on the land, hunting and fishing.

There is a big sea running at Cape James, and it's a problem finding an area to put the plane down and also get out of. I make repeated passes over the cluster of white tents, and a couple of uncommitted approaches among the islands, before choosing a narrow channel with about 180 metres of choppy water. I figure that once the 90-kilogram mechanic and his 23-kilogram tool box are out, I can be off again before reaching the biggest of the rollers at the end of the channel. The water is deep and the wind strong; my anchor doesn't hold, but the Inuit are there in minutes in one of their Montreal canoes. They seem aware of the fragility of an airplane near the rocky coast and quickly pluck the mechanic and his tool box from my flying boat as I anxiously watch the approaching shore. They are loaded and clear of my path in what seems like seconds. I fire up and make my takeoff without further delay.

Some days earlier, a dozen or so of the stone carvers had set off by boat to dig soapstone at Aberdeen Inlet. Terry was a little concerned, as they had a case of dynamite, which they had never used before, with them. Our time would be well spent checking them out while waiting for the mechanic.

Inuit returning after dynamite blast

Aberdeen Inlet is deep, long and sheltered from Hudson Strait. We tie off behind the carvers' Peterhead boat, letting them both weathercock in the wind. Hungry mosquitoes descend in black swarms as soon as we are ashore. The natives protect themselves with hooded parkas as they go about digging soapstone. We have arrived in time; they haven't yet tried to use the dynamite. Terry gives their leader a few lessons. When he is satisfied, we head back towards Cape James. Along the way we stop off at Amadjuak, the old abandoned Hudson's Bay post, situated high above a rocky shore. The tide is receding, so I decide to land a few miles to the west on Boas Lake where I tie the flying boat to drift offshore in the light breeze. We walk over the hills to the lonely post. The proctor's house, store and shed full of coal stand ready for use. The smell of walrus oil still hangs in the air of the skin sheds. The company store's shelves are empty; the pine counter is scratched and worn from years of transactions. A few tokens used in trading lie scattered on the floor. Farther up the hill, near the powder shed, I find three graves: piles of stone marked with weathered wooden crosses, held together with wooden pegs. One cross has fallen over and parted, so I hammer it together with a stone and right it. This is also the site chosen by the arctic explorer Vilhjalmur Stefansson for his ill-conceived plan to domesticate and raise reindeer. The pens can still be seen.

Instruction in the use of dynamite

There is a great deal more to explore, but it is time for Terry and me to pick up the mechanic, left behind at Cape James. The wind has dropped at Teeku Camp. I am able to land in front of the camp in an open bay and tie off behind the repaired Peterhead boat as the men come out to meet us. The mechanic has done his job and got the diesel motor going. We drink cups of strong Eskimo tea served by the women while the men gathered around Terry laugh and joke in their native tongue. The children play with their traditional toys: baby gulls which cannot yet fly—often hugging them to death.

Kaka's son Okituk hands me a small soapstone carving of a Canada goose and says something in Inuktitut. Terry explains: "He gives this to you for helping his father." I ask Terry to tell him that I will always treasure it. Because I cannot conceive of life without art, I like to think that this carving was made with love, that the best carvers would make objects from stone and bone even if a southern market for them did not exist, just as they did in the past.

We drop into one of the fish-filled, freshwater lakes on the way back to Cape Dorset, to wash off the salt water from the plane. This has been one of the most memorable flying days of my month-long stay in the Arctic.

Flying boat tied off behind Peterhead boat

Abandoned Hudson's Bay camp at Amadjuak

Terry Ryan and friends

I drink strong tea in one of the tents with a family I have gotten to know, then go out to find the remains of Parr's old house in the valley. He and his wife abandoned it in 1961, the year before he died. I find the remains: an old, rusty cast-iron stove and an outline in the moss where the house once stood. Terry Ryan has recently told me a delightful story about Parr when he was living at Tessikjakjuak. In 1961, his wife, Eleeshushe, came into Cape Dorset to see the nurse. She said that Parr was not feeling well and described his illness. The nurse prescribed a box of pills to be taken three times daily and said to come back in a week. Eleeshushe returned a week later to report that she had taken all the pills and that Parr was feeling much better.

This is quite understandable if one considers that Parr's mother was an Angakog, a "shaman." Magic must have been an everyday part of his life. Of all the Inuit artists, his raw talent moves me the most. He was born before acculturation and the demands of a southern market. Parr's vision differed little from the time when the ethnologist Franz Boas put paper and pencils into the hands of Inuit hunters in the 1880s. Parr's rough block figures of men and animals, drawn with speed and urgency, are the works of a man not in the act of consciously making art but of a hunter transported, reliving the life he loved before he lost a foot to frostbite. His spirit must be here someplace, maybe splashing in the river playing with his children (Parr fathered many) catching char.

Inuk boys discover Toni's paintings

Keakshook, Toni, Terry Ryan and children

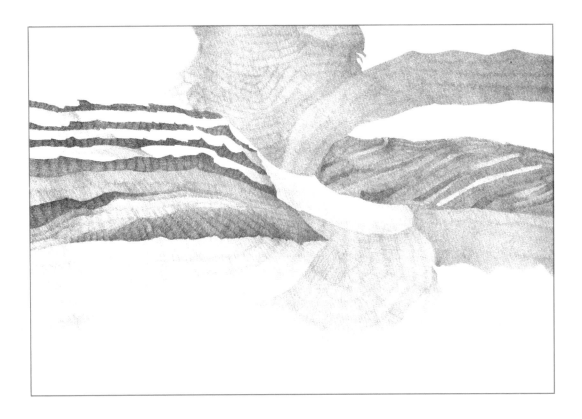

Teeku Camp

Cape Dorset Bay / Cape Dorset Suite
LITHOGRAPH

I pick up my watercolour box and paper and walk up the valley to the lakes and do a couple of watercolours. Five Inuk boys with rifles and a dead rabbit discover me painting and stay to watch. I must have been a strange sight to them. "What am I doing?" they ask. "Should I not be hunting food? Could I eat the paper?" All good questions! They are wonderful company. When I am finished, we all walk back to the camp together. As we descend the valley, I can see that the bay is empty; my flying boat is nowhere to be seen. The tide has receded and where my plane had once rode at anchor, great rocks have grown out of the sea floor. I immediately think that my aircraft has been holed by the rocks and has sunk. As I run to the water's edge, the whole camp comes down and gathers around me. Then, all together, they burst into laughter, many rolling on the moss and holding their stomachs as the tears roll down their round cheeks. It is a big joke on me. Apparently they had all been keeping an eye on the airplane as the tide receded. When I did not return, they took matters into their own hands. They pulled up my anchor, towed the airplane around the south point and into a deep water bay where they anchored it. These are people in touch with nature, its ever-changing conditions and above all in touch with each other, and each other's interest, which now included me. I could not help thinking that if this had happened on English Bay, the whole of Vancouver would have stood and watched my flying boat beat itself to death on the rocks.

AUGUST 13

The days are becoming noticeably shorter; suddenly one morning all the arctic flowers are gone—the little white-petalled diapensia, the purple saxifrage, the Lapland rhododendron—killed by the first frost. It could snow any day now, and the time to leave has arrived. I have made many friends at Cape Dorset, and the whole settlement comes out to see us off. They make me promise to come back during the nice weather in winter! I make a low pass over the tiny crowd, dip my wings, and Cape Dorset slips from sight, a dot on the arctic landscape. Over 200 nautical miles of unfriendly ice-filled water lie ahead.

By the time we reach King Charles Cape, the plane is at 10,000 feet with a magnificent view in all directions. The sea is a pure undiluted ultramarine blue, the colour John Ruskin described as "everlastingly appointed by the Deity to be the source of delight." I can see Terror Point, our first landfall to the west, 190 kilometers away on Southampton Island, and to the north across the Great Plain of Koukdjuak, Foxe Basin, Prince Charles Island and Air Force Island are visible—shining white islands that were not on the map until 1947 when they were spotted by a Canadian Airforce patrol. Distance in the clear arctic air is unimpeded. The compass is up to its usual antics; however, the Coral Harbour beacon comes in strong, and we are further encouraged by a tailwind. Everything is in the green as we fly out from the tip of Foxe Peninsula to cross Foxe Channel. We can laugh at the names on the map such as Bay of God's Good Mercy, Terror Point, Thank God Harbour and Ruin Point—places splendid in isolation rather than a threat.

Ten days earlier I had shipped a rusty drum of nine-year-old Avgas via Nordair to Coral Harbour because that stopover was out of fuel. I could have saved my money: the fuel ship arrived a few days before us. I exchange my old fuel for fresh, and we leave for Rankin Inlet. Weather and visibility are still with us as we cross Neultra Strait. We can look up Roes Welcome Sound to Cape Munn in the north and see Chesterfield Inlet to Baker Lake in the west. But it looks like low cloud to the southwest, and there are scattered clouds below us as we cross Baker Foreland. At Baird Bay it goes from scattered to solid. We drop underneath and follow the beacon across the inlet only to find the hamlet and airstrip totally obscured in fog. I pull up to 1000 feet and fly back and forth over the beacon contemplating a landing in one of the lakes we had crossed 15 miles back, when, like the Red Sea, the fog parts directly over the airstrip, and we are down and safe. I am given a bunk in a miners' barracks, and the women take my wife off somewhere else to sleep.

Moon Over Admiralty Inlet
LITHOGRAPH

Blue Passage/Island Suite
SERIGRAPH

Arctic Shore
SERIGRAPH

Dolman Bay
SERIGRAPH

Inukshuit/Cape Dorset Suite
LITHOGRAPH

AUGUST 14 *Rankin Inlet Lat.62°48'N Long.92°07'W*

I phone the Churchill weather office and get a 2000-foot ceiling, visibility unlimited, with no weather information between. It is clear at Rankin with an offshore breeze. We file a flight plan and leave for Churchill. Within half an hour patches of fog appear and thicken, and as we progress, join forces with the lowering ceiling. It is time for a 180° turn, but just then the sun sparkles momentarily on a patch of water about 10 miles to the east, out in Hudson Bay. I head for it and let down to within 50 feet of the surface. I can see the coast again and Sentry Island; Eskimo Point is just beyond. It is no problem to fly around the few wisps of cloud that come down to touch the water.

As we pass over the little hamlet of Eskimo Point, I can see yellow earth-moving equipment building a runway just beyond. The sky is lighter to the south now, and by the time we reach McConnell River, the ceiling is up to 2000 feet and lifting. We pass over the breeding grounds of millions of Canada geese. They line the lakes and shores of Hudson Bay, but not one is flying. (They have more sense than we do.) East of the Knife River out over Hudson Bay with good visibility, I can see the first stunted trees since leaving them at Fort Chimo on July 8.

When I call Churchill, I feel as if I were coming in from another planet. The controller's voice is clear and strangely comforting as she calls me number two behind a C-5 on a five-mile final approach for runway 33. The runway is one of the longest in the north. It takes time and patience to reach its end staying above the C-5's glide path. (The C-5 being one of the largest military transports on earth, its wake turbulence could cut us in two if we were to fly below its glide path.) From Churchill to Vancouver is a lazy fourteen-hour flight with time out to visit good restaurants along the way.

If there are few adventures left to the Canadian pilot, a flight to the Canadian Arctic remains an absorbing challenge. I value the times when the adrenalin ran free and I felt very much alive, hanging on by a fragile piece of technology, flying in an ancient land, disturbing the silence of the Arctic only momentarily, leaving it to converse with the sky.

Winter Cove/Coast Suite
SERIGRAPH

Darkening Land
SERIGRAPH

Arctic Bay
OIL, 1983

We set off again at 0700 hours. Slow going at first in thick ice with ridging. The MV Arctic has reported 50 nautical miles to the north of us. Our orders from Ottawa are to wait for her in Dundas Harbour, Devon Island. We are in low visibility, whiteout conditions. We come across great flocks of dovekies. These small black birds with white undersides, tiny black bills and rapid whirring wing-beats are all heading for Lancaster Sound with us where they will join up with a third of the thirty million of their species that nest in northwest Greenland.

Throughout our journey in the ice we have been turning up a species of algae that grows on the bottom of the sea ice called epontic algae. Not altogether attractive, it produces a light umber-brown stain in the water when disturbed. The underside of the ice seems to be a perfect growing surface for this algae, which is the bottom of the food chain. The polar bear, only a few metres away on the surface of the ice, is at the top of the food chain. But in that short distance he takes in many contaminants, such as PCBs. One can develop Trichinosis from eating polar bear meat; 60% of the polar bear population carry it. Also, the high concentrations of vitamin A in polar bear's liver makes it lethal for human consumption.

By 1400 hours we have made it through the last of Baffin Bay ice and into clear water on the north side of Lancaster Sound the Parry Channel, establishing a record for being the first ship to enter Lancaster Sound this early in the year. The MV Arctic radios her position 100 nautical miles northwest of us, pushing into strong winds and packing ice. We stick our ship into a large pan of ice off Dundas Harbour on Devon Island to wait for her.

Snow showers occasionally obscure the land. I am grateful to have a sturdy ship beneath me. Had I chosen to fly my own airplane, it would have been white knuckles all the way. An unexpected multiplicity of climates created by the cold land and warmer seas is what the pilot has to contend with up here. Between whiteouts I get a good view of the Cunningham Mountains on Devon Island — which I last painted eleven years ago — and got off seven watercolours. The whiteness of these mountains that transcend space still fools the eye. Mountains turn out not to be mountains but standing waves of lenticular clouds as white as the driven snow at their centre. To observe the light of these opal cones of cloud and mountain can put one into a state of benign catalepsy.

After supper with the captain, Claude and I gave a talk on our work to the officers and crew. At midnight I return to the bridge. The sun is dancing on the hills; pearl grey clouds hang in the valleys, and the sky is filled with ice-crystal rainbows. Clouds that could be carved from rock hang low over Cunningham Glacier. We are only a kilometre or two offshore.

My paint box and board are where I left them eight hours ago, so I do a watercolour of the midnight sun casting its soft shadows on the snow — a scene of both reality and fantasy saturated in a wonderful light that I and my brush can only approximate; it is intimately an order of purity that is impossible to achieve in pigment.

Before turning in, I spend some time in silent contemplation of the moonscape before me. We have slowly and irresistibly snatched a path to this place, the eastern entrance to Lancaster Sound and

ABOARD THE CCGS *DES GROSEILLIERS*

An Artist and a Poet Journey to
Lancaster Sound: 1986

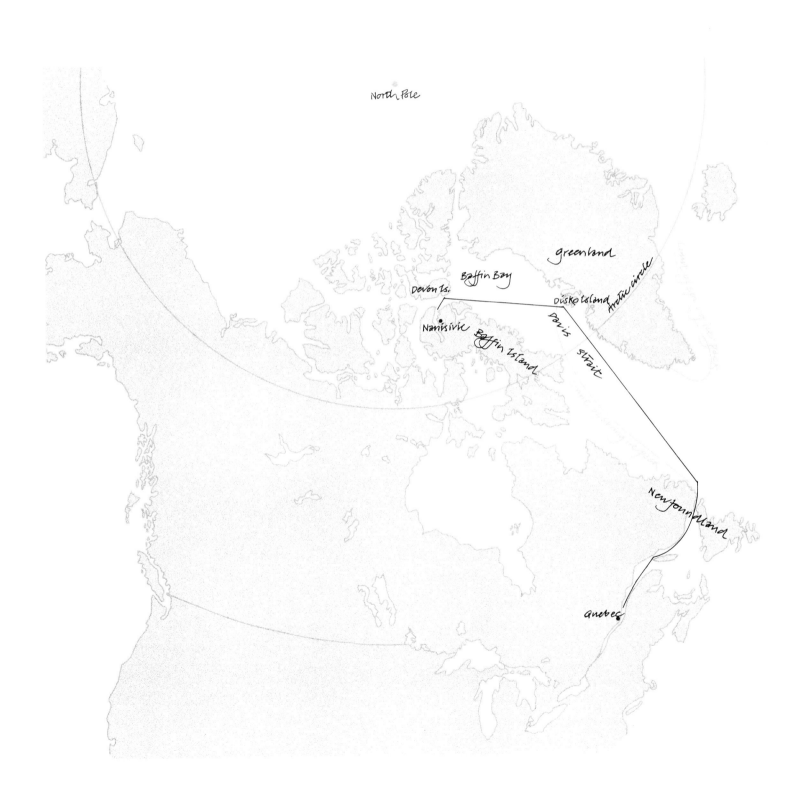

North Pole

greenland

Baffin Bay

Devon Is.

Disko Island

Arctic circle

Nanisivic

Baffin Island

Davis Strait

Newfoundland

Quebec

In the spring of 1983 I had a fortuitous meeting with Quebec poet Claude Péloquin; the result was a happy collaboration on three hand-produced books. We were eager to do another book, this time with the Arctic landscape as inspiration, and began casting about for a way to get to the North. Two years were to pass before political events opened the door.

In the summer of 1985 the United States announced plans for one of its flagships to penetrate the Northwest Passage as if it were, as the Toronto *Globe and Mail* expressed it, "an American Lake." I immediately wrote to three Canadian federal ministers—Secretary of State for External Affairs Joe Clark, Minister of Transport Don Mazankowski, Minister of Indian Affairs and Northern Development David Crombie—suggesting that a working trip into the region by a painter and a writer would confirm Canada's cultural sovereignty over these waters. All the ministers' replies were encouraging, and six months later, in May 1986, Claude and I received word that we might join the crew of the Coast Guard icebreaker *Des Groseilliers* heading for Lancaster Sound. Two days later we were underway.

Escorting the M/V Arctic *in the Eastern Lead, Baffin Bay*
WATERCOLOUR, SPRING 1986

MAY 22

We set sail at 1400 hours from the Canadian Coast Guard docks, Quebec City, on a new, clean class 3 icebreaker, the CCGS *Des Groseilliers*. Capt. Claude Guimont is a man of great warmth and humour, and the officers and men obviously like him. It is an all-French ship; all signs are in French only, even the sign over my bunk instructing me to master station #5 *(postes d'urgence poste de Rassemblement #5)*. If the ship goes down will only the French-speaking be saved?

This is an important voyage for several reasons. It is the earliest time of year that a Canadian icebreaker has ever attempted to reach Lancaster Sound, the eastern entrance to the Northwest Passage. It is also something of an experimental voyage, for we are to assist the commercial icebreaker MV *Arctic* to Nanisivik near Arctic Bay in Adams Sound (Lat. 73°00'N Long. 83°30'W) off Admiralty Inlet.

Claude, crazy poet that he is, has kept the officers entertained all day and evening, but in spite of this delightful distraction, we manage to get under way. CBC TV's news crew has joined us and remain on board part way down the St. Laurence River before our helicopter returns them to Quebec City in time to show us on the 10:00 P.M. news. There is no way we could have left silently with Claude aboard. He fires off news releases to Radio-T.V. and Canadian Press. I would have preferred to sail off silently into the night. However, as much as I distrust all media, I know that if we are to make an effective cultural sovereignty trip, it needs to be publicized.

Captain Guimont has kindly provided us with a large forward cabin below the wheelhouse on the main deck, with two bunks, a lower and an upper. The night before sailing, Claude was out on the town until 4 A.M. but, tired after my long flight from Vancouver, I returned to the ship early, made the cabin shipshape and appropriated the lower bunk. After a few days at sea I succumbed to Claude's grumbling each time he climbed into the upper bunk, and switched with him.

The captain has allowed me to set up and paint my watercolours on the bridge, and has offered the use of the helicopter whenever I wish to accompany the ice observer or to go along when the helicopter has business ashore.

MAY 24   *Lat.51°30'N Long.56°00'W*

We pass through the Strait of Belle Isle under blue sky and in calm sea; low silver clouds hug the coast of Labrador. It is a good day to get out my watercolours, which I do in the afternoon. I paint the coast and clouds and a lone passing iceberg from the port side of the bridge. Captain Guimont is very interested in my activity and orders the helmsman to steer so that our first iceberg will be on the port side, a better view for painting. He then orders the carpenter to cut me a larger drawing board, one I can wedge beneath the window like a sloping desk, leaving my hands free. But for today, I paint while balancing the lid of my box on the rail with my paper taped to it.

We are leaving land now and heading for the eastern lead off the west coast of Greenland. (A lead is a passage through the sea ice navigable by a surface vessel.) In the past two days we have spotted many whales close to our ship and today we pass three killer whales. Each morning Claude is up by 0500 hours writing busily; he only needs six hours' sleep. A gentle swell rocks us to sleep at night as we head north into the North Atlantic.

CCGS *Des Groseilliers*

Toni Onley, Claude Péloquin

*Anse-Amour, Labrador, Strait of
Belle Isle*
WATERCOLOUR, MAY 24, 1986

Baffin Bay, Midnight
WATERCOLOUR, MAY 24, 1986

MAY 25 *Lat.65°00'N Long.56°00'W*

We are out of sight of land under grey sky; our ship, shaped like an egg, rolls and pitches in the swells. Many of the crew are sick, and by 0500 Claude is hanging onto the rail above the wheelhouse getting wet with sea spray. I hunker down in my bunk and read. We are accompanied by sea birds: arctic terns on their 22,000-mile-long migration from the Antarctic to nest in the Canadian Arctic; fulmars, stiff winged, ridge-flying the waves and the ternlike Ross' gull. We will follow the eastern lead 65 nautical miles off the Greenland coast and by noon will pass through Lat. 65°N Long. 56'W into open water.

MAY 26 *Lat.65°00'N Long.55°00'W*

The sea has calmed to a gentle swell. An iceberg on the horizon fooled the captain who thought for a moment it was a sailing ship under full white sails. I too was fooled because it pitched in the swell like a ship. We are still out of sight of land but are followed by more and more seabirds. At one point we are joined by a skua flying faster than all the other birds. There are now flocks of black-legged kittiwakes, and two thick-billed murres join us, flapping their wings frantically to keep up. They are a long way from shore.

We receive a message at 1100 hours from the MV *Arctic* that she is two days behind us, just coming through the Strait of Belle Isle. We will wait for her when we reach the ice tomorrow off the Greenland coast, a pause that will give me a chance to do some watercolours.

Iceberg, Davis Strait
WATERCOLOUR, MAY 26, 1986

"A crack will slowly open ahead for maybe a mile. Our ship is fitted with a bow knife which acts like a glass cutter."

MAY 27 *Lat.69°00'N Long.56°00'W*

At 0730 hours we sail into a forest of large icebergs. Clouds race across the sea, casting shadows over the floes. Colours are constantly moving and changing. The reflection of ice on the low clouds makes an eerie, pale yellow light. Icebergs shaped like giant sculptures change their form as we glide past them. Stark white when the sun strikes them, they turn translucent cobalt blue or emerald green when a cloud shadow creeps across them. Then they dissolve like ghosts into a snow shower only to reappear, now differently shaped, continuing their slow journey to the North Atlantic.

We are about 60 nautical miles southwest of Disko Island, Greenland. Just when we thought we were all alone, three large Danish fishing vessels appear on the horizon dragging the bottom for cod. We are in shallow water, and many of the largest icebergs are grounded here until such time as they dissolve sufficiently to continue their journey. I paint the ever-changing seascape of ice and blue-black water from 0730 to 1700 hours, filling sheet after sheet until I am too tired to stand.

The ship's carpenter has finished cutting me a metre-square plywood drawing board which I wedge under the window; it slopes down on a perfect angle for painting watercolours. Everyone on the bridge is distracted from the serious business of navigating through the ice by the presence of a painter frantically wielding a great Chinese goat hair brush trying to get down the exact gradation of light as it rapidly changes. The subject is always a jump ahead of me.

Drifting Ice, Baffin Bay
WATERCOLOUR, MAY 27, 1986

Claude has had a wondrous day and claims he will never again be the same. He writes a poem to that effect. Tonight Captain Guimont will stick our ship into the ice pack. Then we will wait three days for the *Arctic* to arrive so that we can escort her the rest of the way to Nanisivik. There is no hurry as we cannot enter Admiralty Inlet before June 1; otherwise we would disturb the narwhals giving birth in May. (Apparently breaking the ice is very disruptive to sea mammals during this period.) But my reading tells me that narwhals mate in April and calve in June and July. Captain Guimont is rightfully worried.

Drifting Cloud and Iceberg, Baffin Bay
WATERCOLOUR, MAY 27, 1986

Iceberg Drifting in Baffin Bay
WATERCOLOUR, SPRING 1986

Devon Island from Lancaster Sound
WATERCOLOUR, JUNE 3, 1986

Midnight Sun, Baffin Bay
WATERCOLOUR, MAY 24, 1986

Iceberg in the Eastern Lead,
Baffin Bay
OIL, 1986

In the Eastern Lead, Baffin Bay
OIL, 1987

*Cape Charles Yorke, Borden
Peninsula, Baffin Island*
OIL, 1986

Eastern Entrance, Lancaster Sound.
WATERCOLOUR, 1986

Svartenhuk, Greenland
WATERCOLOUR, MAY 30, 1986

Kap Cranstown, Greenland
WATERCOLOUR, MAY 30, 1986

MAY 29

The sky has cleared. I am outside in shirtsleeves all day. The distant clouds lift, and Disko Island comes into view 80 kilometres east of us. Cliffs the colour of indigo rise 300 metres out of the spring ice into a 1900-metre ice cap glowing pink. Distance is deceptive in the clear arctic air. I am able to do two watercolours of the distinct features of Disko Island. Claude commandeered one I did of the midnight sun. He is so delighted with my work that I give him another one: light exploding out of an iceberg. Claude has composed a poem on my watercolour paper for Captain Guimont; I paint the ice floe over it and dedicate it to him. The captain is profoundly moved by his gift.

For a time today I stop painting and simply watch the veil of colours playing over the sky and ice with soft pink Disko Island looming out of the white sea ice. This is what Turner called "the dewy light on which the eye dwells so completely enthralled, when it seeks for its liberty." He continues, "[I] think it a sacrilege to pierce the mystic shell of colour in search of form." The sky is pale cerulean blue rising into a dusty raw umber on which pearl grey clouds edged in lamp black and ultramarine blue drift silently, creating cobalt violet shadows over the ice. Distant ice becomes a soft pale ochre. This is a mystic world, receiving and emitting rays of light, floating on a blue-black sea. We in our little shell-like ship are locked into the ice and drift with the changing scene, pirouetting ever so slowly, as if to the time of a celestial clock. In the space of twenty-four hours I see and paint 360°. The sun swings in a giant arc to the south of our position, like a pendulum.

Iceberg, Baffin Bay
WATERCOLOUR, SPRING 1986

*Midnight Sun, Dundas Harbour,
Devon Island*
WATERCOLOUR, JUNE 3, 1986

Lead in the Ice, Lancaster Sound
WATERCOLOUR, SPRING 1986

MAY 30 *Lat.69°15'N Long.54°20'W*

Captain Guimont moves the ship to within 20 nautical miles of Disko Island. I like to think he does this so that I can get a better view of the Greenland landscape. The views I painted yesterday of Disko were in fact a mirage of an island floating in the sky. These mirages are so sharp that I am easily fooled, as were many early explorers such as Robert Peary, John Ross and Charles Francis Hall, all of whom plotted new lands that were later proved to be ephemera.

We will wait here for the MV *Arctic*. Captain Guimont tells me this is the most beautiful weather he has ever experienced in Baffin Bay. It is warm in the sun with not a breath of wind. A rich blue-black sky of snow showers moves across the horizon and reflects in the water between the ice floes turning it an inky indigo. A fat seal lazes on a small floe a few feet off our bow. I paint watercolours from 0800 until 2100 hours, stopping only a half hour for supper. The ship slowly shifting, the light and cloud shadows slowly shifting, provide me with continual subjects, sheet after sheet, until I have piled up fourteen watercolours—the most I have ever painted nonstop in my entire life.

Dundas Harbour, Devon Island

Calm in Baffin Bay

M/V *Arctic*, Entrance of Admiralty Inlet

Toni Onley

Claude Péloquin, Captain Claude Guimont
Toni Onley in the Wheelhouse

I think of Samuel G. Grosswell, second lieutenant aboard Robert M'Clure's ship *Investigator*. He was a remarkably gifted watercolour painter but managed to complete only eight watercolours on a journey that started at Barrow Point on August 2, 1850, through the Northwest Passage, arriving at this very spot off Disko Island September 6, 1854. To be fair, the *Investigator* was abandoned at Bay of Mercy on Banks Island in 1851. Grosswell spent three years in weather so cold it would freeze a watercolour brush to the paper. By comparison I work in modern comfort in a heated wheelhouse.

The MV *Arctic* arrives at 1800 hours, steaming between us and Greenland, and we sail off north together in open water. Sometime tonight we will come to the end of the lead and enter pack ice; then we will both head west through it to Lancaster Sound. For two hours this evening we sailed through a sculpture court of magnificent icebergs, the sun low in the sky lighting up deep-cut facets within them, "like jewelry from the grave" as Elizabeth Bishop says in her poem "The Imaginary Iceberg." I shot thirty-six slides. Being on the bridge was like being in a space ship, racing low over the surface of the moon and through its valleys.

MAY 31 *Lat. 72°00'N Long. 63°00'W*

We reach the end of the open water along the Greenland coast by noon. The *Arctic* leads the way as we enter solid ice, about a metre thick at this point. Two polar bears move in a slow lope alongside of us in search of seal but also with catlike curiosity at this unfamiliar red-and-white beast moving so effortlessly through the ice. The colour has completely changed today. Pale translucent cerulean blue, the icebergs are almost indistinguishable from the sky; they could be clouds ready to break free and fly away. Our navigator with his sextant measured some 90 metres high —great floating islands.

Our helicopter pilot has brought back a sizable chunk of clear ice from one of the flat-topped icebergs we passed today. We will have it in our drinks this evening. The ice will continually release its trapped 2000-year-old air as it bubbles and pops in our 10-year-old scotch. Over such drinks the mind wanders back to some of the tragic voyages of exploration in this area during the eighteenth and nineteenth centuries. They must have fired the imagination of Europeans at that time. In a way, Turner was to anticipate the Franklin disaster with his 1842 painting "Peace – Burial at Sea."

Pyramid Iceberg in the Ice Pack,
Baffin Bay
WATERCOLOUR, JUNE 1, 1986

Sea Ice at Ship Point,
Admiralty Inlet, Baffin Island
WATERCOLOUR, JUNE 4, 1986 (left)

The Arctic is a fitting subject for the manifestation of the sublime—the representation, in Edmund Burke's words, of "whatever is in any sort terrible" or, as William Hazlitt wrote, "The artist delights to go back to the first chaos of the world, or to that state of things, when the waters were separated from dry land, and light from darkness." The luminous communication of light seems to make acute observers of everyone on board the *Des Groseilliers*; with few exceptions they all make statements on the profundity of the landscape. Everyone here has a story to tell, of how it can draw you in, close behind you and snuff you out! As Barry Lopez observed in his excellent book *Arctic Dreams*: "Its power derives from the tension between its obvious beauty and its capacity to take life." Such observations come about like a natural reflex, as involuntary as a sneeze.

It is entirely possible that some of the men of the Franklin expedition brought with them images of Turner's paintings as well as contemporary poems to help them translate this landscape. We know they brought West End plays of the day to help while away the long dark winters in the ice. Might they not also have brought copies of Wordsworth and Coleridge?

JUNE 1 *Lat.72°25'N Long.71°00'W*

Since entering the ice yesterday we have made amazing progress. The leads all seem to open in the general direction of our course. Occasionally the ship has ground to a halt when we come upon a pressure ridge. Generally the ice is first year from freezing (it started last September or early October) and up to two metres thick. The amazing thing to watch is the point at which we leave a lead and enter a pan of this solid ice; a crack will slowly open ahead for maybe a mile. Our ship is fitted with a bow knife which acts like a glass cutter. Once the crack starts, the break seems as inevitable as the breaking of glass. This ship does not rise up on the ice and crash down through it using the ship's weight to make the break, as does the *John A. MacDonald* or the *Louis S. St. Laurent*. It simply displaces several square miles of ice to one or both sides, like moving a giant log boom. The water is cold, below -2°C and as new ice forms in the leads, it assumes the black-grey colour and texture of emery cloth. The new ice breaks ahead of us in a geometric, battlement-shaped pattern called finger rafting that looks almost man-made. Among the leads today we see many walrus with their young. A pod of a dozen narwhals swims ahead of us in the open water. Flocks of timid dovekies fly off in a cloud before we get too near.

It is impossible to paint today with all the movement—crashing, pounding, backing up and ramming of ridges. At times it is even hard to stand upright. So that we could all get a little sleep, the captain parked in a lead last night and shut the ship down from 12 midnight until 0500 hours this morning. For most of the day I searched the horizon from the wheelhouse with my binoculars, looking for signs of life on the sea ice. We cross polar bear tracks—some fresh, some old; some telling a story, some making no sense. I saw two fresh sets of tracks converge into a single trail. Could a male have come across female tracks and instinctively followed her? The tracks lead off in a straight line as far as I can see. Perhaps they read the sky as I do for a "water blink," that dark patch of blue-black sky indicating open water below, and maybe seal. Other tracks wander like a drunken sailor. We have seen few seal today which could account for the polar bears heading to better hunting grounds. A polar bear would have to be hungry to tackle the walrus we see here. Apparently bears fear only killer whales and walrus.

Spring Ice, Lancaster Sound
WATERCOLOUR, JUNE 11, 1986 (left)

Baffin Bay
WATERCOLOUR, MAY 30, 1986

*Cape Charles Yorke from
Admiralty Inlet*
WATERCOLOUR, 1986

Ice Islands, Baffin Bay
OIL, 1987

Crocker Bay, Devon Island
OIL, 1986

JUNE 2 *Lat.74°00'N Long.76°00'W*

It is bright and warm in the sun. I spend all morning in the wheelhouse painting in spite of the vibration and rolling in the ice. The ship's rolling has given my watercolours an impromptu freedom of touch. We are now into solid old ice with not a lead on the horizon. The helicopter has been out twice this morning looking for an easier route, but there is none. We must crash through ridge after ridge, sometimes backing up and ramming four times to get through a tough one.

Brodeur Peninsula, Lancaster Sound
WATERCOLOUR, JUNE 3, 1986

The MV *Arctic*, at her captain's request, has been left behind to make her own way from the Greenland coast to Lancaster Sound. This I cannot understand as it is the mission of the *Des Groseilliers* to assist her. However, the *Arctic* is a class 4 icebreaker and we are a class 3, and although we are in radio contact, the chances of our returning to help her will not be likely. She is moving slower looking for heavy ice to test her new bow. She could have had good ice trials without going out of her way just by coming with us! She is now in heavy ice 25 nautical miles northeast of us off Cape York, Greenland. I am reminded of Capt. Robert M'Clure's decision not to wait twenty-four hours for Capt. Richard Collinson at Kotzebue Sound, Alaska, in July 1850. M'Clure in the HMS *Investigator* impatiently took off without any backup to enter Amundsen Gulf and met eventual disaster on Banks Island. Our ships are better equipped to go it alone.

Lemieux Point, Dundas Harbour,
Devon Island
WATERCOLOUR, JUNE 3, 1986

Cape Crawford from
Admiralty Inlet
WATERCOLOUR, 1986

The *Arctic* is proving quite remarkable in her new bow trials. For a time, two days ago, it looked as if we would have to escort the motor vessel, because her two high-frequency radios blew up, but our technician flew over and made one radio out of the two broken ones. It worked!

We are taking a hell of a pounding, engines going full bore as we creep through the ice, sometimes at only one knot. From time to time the engineer phones the wheelhouse to say he's shutting her down—"smoke in the engine room." It does not seem to worry Captain Guimont who laughs and says, "It's usual." The ice blocks, which hit the screws, send continuous shudders through the ship. But between the ice ridges I have developed enough sea (or ice) legs to stand at my drawing board and do some very loose watercolours of the delicate pale shadows in the trapped icebergs and ice ridges—the pale cobalt blue tones on the large expansive pans of ice, the sharp whites on the sides of vertical ridges, and the deep thalo green shadows in the recesses between the blocks of ice. The navigator says, "There is nothing to paint; all is white." "Nothing is my forte," I reply. In Kandinsky's view, white was the symbol of "a world from which all colours as material attributes have disappeared." In *Concerning the Spiritual in Art* he wrote, "There comes a great silence which materially represented is like a cold, indestructible wall going on into the infinite. White, therefore, acts upon our psyche as a great, absolute silence. . . . It is not a dead silence, but one pregnant with possibilities. White has the appeal of nothingness that is before birth, of the world in the ice age."

By 1400 hours Bylot Island comes into view 80 kilometres to the southwest, but the ice is getting thicker and one of our six engines has packed it in. Now that we are closer to land we see more and more polar bears. One, its face covered in blood, has a seal torn apart, red blood splashed over the fresh snow. Arctic foxes will not be far behind to clean up on the leavings. We see many fox tracks but no fox. The fox needs the bear: the bear eats only the blubber, the fox the rest. One big polar bear jumps into the water in a lead covered with new ice, swimming like an icebreaker, bringing his big jaw down on the thin ice ahead of him to break it. Claude was in the helicopter overhead and had a good view: from only two metres away he could see the bear's teeth.

We have shut down for the night so the engineers can fit the oil pump on No. 6 engine.

Lead in the Spring Ice,
Lancaster Sound
OIL, 1987

Disko Island, Greenland
WATERCOLOUR MAY, 30, 1986

Iceberg off Godhavn, Greenland
WATERCOLOUR, MAY 27, 1986

JUNE 4 *Lat. 74°28'N Long. 82°25'W*

We spent last night in the ice at Dundas Harbour. I spend the morning painting the Cunningham Mountains again before we move off across Lancaster Sound to wait for the *Arctic* at Cape Joy, Borden Peninsula. I paint myself snow blind in the afternoon sun, staring at the magnificent crimson cliffs across the white expanse of ridging ice of Admiralty Inlet. The tough ice of the inlet, which has not moved this spring, is two metres thick, thicker in the ridges. We are now only 50 nautical miles from our destination, Nanisivic. This will be the real test for the *Arctic*. At 1700 hours she is abeam about 20 nautical miles west and moving very slowly. It is something of a miracle of modern engineering that she has made it this far. Her stern is not strengthened so she cannot back up in the ice to take a run at it as we do. She can only lean on it until it breaks, and she does this very well.

The wind shifted in the night and has brought out pack-ice from the entrance to Admiralty Inlet clearing the way for us to get as far as Cape Joy before we will be breaking fresh ice again. The cape is named for Inspector Joy of the RCMP who patrolled this area in the 1920s and thirties. A.Y. Jackson, who travelled with the inspector aboard the *Beothic* in 1936, recalled in his book *A Painter's Country* a story Joy told "about a trip he had made to Melville Island in 1929 when he ran out of supplies and looked up an old cache put down for Franklin in 1852. There he found raisins, canned mutton and carrots, in prime condition, and some woollen goods, which he was still wearing."

Bluff Head, Borden Peninsula,
Baffin Island
WATERCOLOUR, JUNE 4, 1986

Fort Chimo, *see* Kuujjuak
Fort McKenzie 56° 50'N 68° 57'W
Foxe Basin 67° 00'N 77° 00'W
Foxe Island, West 64° 17'N 75° 45'W
Foxe Peninsula 64° 40'N 77° 00'W
Frobisher Bay, *see* Iqaluit
Godhavn, *see* Qeqertarshuaq
Greenland, *see* Kalaallit
Hazen Lake 81° 48'N 71° 15'W
Herschel, Cape 78° 37'N 74° 40'W
Hudson Bay 60° 00'N 85° 00'W
Hudson Strait 62° 30'N 72° 00'W
Humbolt Glacier 79° 30'N 65° 00'W
Isabella, Cape 78° 20'N 75° 00'W
Iqaluit 63° 45'N 68° 35'W
James, Cape 64° 22'N 74° 08'W
Jones Sound 76° 05'N 85° 00'W
Joy, Cape 73° 40'N 83° 10'W
Kalaallit 72° 00'N 40° 00'W
Kane Basin 79° 30'N 69° 30'W
Kaniapskan River 57° 00'N 69° 10'W
Kaujuitoq 74° 41'N 94° 54'W
Koartac 61° 03'N 69° 38'W
Kokspak River 57° 45'N 69° 20'W
Kuujjuak 58° 06'N 68° 26'W
Labrador 54° 00'N 62° 00'W
Lac le Moyne 56° 43'N 68° 42'W
Lancaster Sound 74° 10'N 85° 00'W
Little Cornwallis Island 75° 35'N 96° 30'W
Lookout Island 45° 33'N 80° 30'W
Mercy, Bay of God's (now Mercy Bay) 74° 15'N 118° 10'W
Meta Incognita Peninsula 62° 55'N 68° 40'W
Mittimatalik 72° 47'N 77° 00'W
Nanisivic 73° 04'N 84° 30'W
Navy Board Inlet 73° 13'N 80° 52'W
Newfoundland 52° 00'N 56° 00'W
Northumberland Island 77° 23'N 72° 00
Northwater 75° 30'N 75° 00
Nottingham Island 63° 20'N 78° 00'W
Nutak 57° 28'N 61° 52'W
Observation Cove 62° 25'N 69° 06'W
Otelunk Lake 56° 10'N 68° 15'W
Parry Channel 74° 30'N 84° 00'W
Payne Bay 60° 00'N 70° 00'W
Pentecôte, Lac 49° 52'N 67° 20'W
Philpots Island 74° 55'N 79° 45'W
Pim Island 78° 44'N 74° 25'W

Pond Inlet, *see* Mittimatalik
Port de Boucherville 63°07'N 77°56'W
Prince Charles Island 67°30'N 76°00'W
Prince Leopold Island 74°02'N 90°00'W
Pullen Strait 74°25'N 96°20'W
Qaanaaq 77°29'N 69°21'W
Qeqertarshuag 69°15'N 53°33'W
Rankin Inlet 62°48'N 92°07'W
Resolute Bay, *see* Kaujuitoq
Sabourin Lake 51°22'N 94°47'W
St. Irénée 47°35'N 70°12'W
Salisbury Island 63°30'N 77°00'W
Schefferville 54°48'N 66°48'W
Sept-Îles 50°13'N 66°16'W
Smith Sound 78°25'N 73°50'W
Southampton Island 64°30'N 84°00'W
Sugluk 62°13'N 75°40'W
Tanquary Fiord 80°00'N 79°00'W
Teeky Camp 64°16'N 74°46'W
Terror Point 64°05'N 80°55'W
Thank God Harbour 81°36'N 61°10
Thule, *see* Qaanaaq
Tiercel Island 59°00'N 69°00'W
Ungava Bay 59°30'N 67°30'W
Ungava Peninsula 60°00'N 74°00'W
Wakeham Bay 72°00'N 61°40'W
Warrender, Cape 74°28'N 81°40'W
Wellington Channel 75°00'N 93°00'W
Wolstenholme Island 76°35'N 70°00'W
York, Kap (Cape) 75°95'N 66°30'W

WATERCOLOURS

130   Svartenhuk, Greenland, 28x38 cm

131   Kap Cranstown, Greenland, 28x38 cm

132   Iceberg, Baffin Bay, 38x57 cm

132   Midnight Sun, Dundas Harbour, Devon Island, 38x57 cm

133   Lead in the Ice, Lancaster Sound, 28x38 cm

136   Sea Ice at Ship Point, Admiralty Inlet, Baffin Island, 28x38 cm

137   Pyramid Iceberg in the Ice Pack, Baffin Bay, 28x38 cm

138   Spring Ice, Lancaster Sound, 38x57 cm

139   Baffin Bay, 28x38 cm

140   Cape Charles Yorke from Admiralty Inlet, 38x57 cm

142   Brodeur Peninsula, Lancaster Sound, 28x38 cm

143   Lemieux Point, Dundas Harbour, Devon Island, 28x38 cm

143   Cape Crawford from Admiralty Inlet, 38x57 cm

146   Floating Ice, Parry Channel, 28x38 cm

146   Iceberg in the Pack Ice, Baffin Bay, 28x38 cm

148   Midnight Sun, Baffin Bay, 28x38 cm

149   Ship Point, Admiralty Inlet, Baffin Island, 28x38 cm

150   Disko Island, Greenland, 28x38 cm

150   Iceberg off Godhavn, Greenland, 38x57 cm

151   Bluff Head, Borden Peninsula, Baffin Island, 28x38 cm

154   Crocker Bay, Devon Island, 38x57 cm

OILS

7   Cape Herschel, 51x61 cm

24   Iceberg, Eclipse Sound, Baffin Bay, 51x61 cm

29   Passing Iceberg, 51x61 cm

42   Iceberg, Eclipse Sound, 90x104 cm

43   Glacial Boulder, 51x61 cm

46   Glacier, Navy Board Inlet, 51x61 cm

49   Whale Bone, Thule Site, Brooman Point, 51x61 cm

96   Eskimo Point, 51x61 cm

101   Parr's Camp, Cape Dorset, 51x61 cm

113   Arctic Bay, 76x102 cm

128   Iceberg in the Eastern Lead, Baffin Bay, 76x102 cm

129   In the Eastern Lead, Baffin Bay, 168x244 cm

129   Cape Charles Yorke, Borden Peninsula, Baffin Island, 76x102 cm

140   Ice Islands, Baffin Bay, 76x102 cm

141   Crocker Bay, Devon Island, 76x102 cm

145   Lead in the Spring Ice, Lancaster Sound, 76x102 cm

SERIGRAPHS

10   Abandoned Bay, 28x38 cm, Edition 44

36   Winter Shore, 28x38 cm, Edition 40

41   Franklin's Last Winter Camp, 28x38 cm, Edition 35

45   Glacial Boulder/Western Suite, 28x38 cm, Edition 45

53   Greenland, 28x38 cm, Edition 33

56   Iceberg, Baffin Bay/Arctic Suite, 28x38 cm, Edition 60

Boas, Franz. *The Central Eskimo*
    Washington, D.C.: United States Bureau of American Ethnology.
    Sixth Annual Report, 1884–1885.

Bull, John, and John Farrand, Jr. *The Audubon Society
    Field Guide to North American Birds, Eastern Region.*
    New York: Alfred A. Knopf, 1977.

Eber, Dorothy. *Pitseolak: Pictures Out of My Life.*
    Toronto: Oxford University Press, 1973.

Gowing, Lawrence. *Turner: Imagination and Reality.*
    New York: Doubleday & Co., 1966.

Irving, Laurence. *Arctic Life of Birds and Mammals.*
    New York: Springer-Verlag, 1972.

Lopez, Barry. *Arctic Dreams: Imagination and
    Desire in a Northern Landscape.*
    New York: Charles Scribner's Sons, 1986.

Miertsching, Johann. *Frozen Ships: The Arctic Diary of
    Johann Miertsching 1850–1854.*
    Toronto: Macmillan of Canada, 1967.

Mirsky, Jeannette. *To the Arctic!: The Story of Northern
    Exploration from Earliest Times to the Present.*
    Chicago: University of Chicago Press, 1970.

Mowat, Farley. *The Polar Passion.*
    Toronto: McClelland & Stewart, 1973.

Müller, Fritz. *The Living Arctic.*
    Toronto: Methuen, 1981.

Patterson, Nancy-Lou. *Canadian Native Art.*
    Don Mills, Ont.: Collier-Macmillan, 1973.

Swinton, George, and James Houston. *Sculpture/Inuit.*
    Toronto: University of Toronto Press, 1971.

Wilton, Andrew. *Turner and the Sublime.*
    London, Eng.: British Museum Publications, 1980.

Woodford, James. *The Violated Vision:
    the Rape of Canada's North.*
    Toronto: McClelland & Stewart, 1972.

All photos by Toni Onley except:
Robert Keziere Page 77
Iwao Matsuo Pages 17, 84
Robert Murray Pages 17, 80, 110
Tessa Macintosh Pages 86, 87, 92